I0520723

The 3:16 Challenge

Life Changing Scriptures @ Your Fingertips

A Biblical Study for Believers

Volume Two

Reverend Danielle Aly'ce Rome-Briggs

Copyright © 2025 * All Rights Reserved

No part of this book may be reproduced in any form without the written permission of the publisher.

All Scripture Quotations, unless otherwise specified are taken from the King James Version of the Bible.

*****Fourth Printing*****
ISBN 979-8-9940739-0-2
Voice of Rehoboth Publishing
Woodson Terrace, MO. 63134
(314) 764 - 5168
dsbdr@hotmail.com

Preface

The word of God is given for guidance in our daily lives. We find inspiration, strength, wisdom, and comfort in the God-inspired words. We are led to them in the still of the night when we are engulfed in a flood of tears. They speak comfort, peace, and the assurance that we are loved by our Almighty Father. The word of God is good for all that we encounter in the course of our daily lives as we strive to live worthy of the calling to which we have been called.

II Timothy 3:16 *All scripture is given by inspiration of God, and is profitable for doctrine, for reproof, for correction, for instruction in righteousness...*

Yet there are some scriptures that resonate with us so powerfully that their very place in the word comforts us as we whisper to ourselves their places - 3:16.

Throughout the Bible that one scriptural address has meant so much to believers - 3:16. When we recall the words found at **John 3:16** we know beyond the shadow of a doubt that we are loved in the most divinely profound way. God loved us so much that He gave His Son, Jesus Christ, as the once-for-all sacrificial offering for our sins. Is there anything greater? Can there be any words that minister more powerfully? Is there a more staggering truth to be found? I dare say that there are truths of equal magnitude for the believer and many can be found at the same familiar address in scripture - 3:16.

The Bible contains 66 books and of those 48 of them have verses at the 3:16 address. I was astounded by the realization that many of our foundational scriptures are 3:16s. I wondered why and how they came to reside there, the same address on different streets if you will. It suddenly became so obvious - we know how to get to the places that are most significant in our lives. The landmarks of our hearts - church, home, grandma's house - we know how to get there with our eyes closed. God has given us the same ability to nurture our spirit's by giving us 3:16. Some, when we encounter those trials, need encouragement, are longing to be strengthened, are in dire straits and require wisdom; we can go to familiar ground - 3:16 - and find just what we need.

As you read this text, take your time and allow the word and the teaching to minister to your heart and spirit. Do not rush, take your time with this text, your bible, and your journal - write what the Holy Spirit is saying to you. I have studied the scriptures in context, not only providing that key 3:16 verse, but looking at the context and setting the stage for a clarity of understanding. I have also studied the meanings of keywords that were pivotal to the message, including the definitions in the ancient languages, either Hebrew or Greek. As I read the bible it is not a casual experience for me, I truly want to understand so I tend to be quite diligent in my study. That was my approach in writing this book that God placed in my heart so many years ago. When he said the timing was right to go forth, all the tools were at my disposal and I set my hands to this great work. I pray that reading this text will enliven your faith. I challenge you to allow the scriptures to teach you godly principles from antiquity which will strengthen you on your faith journey today.

Yours in Ministry,
Dani Rome-Briggs

Foreword

I'm privileged to write this forward. My perspective of the author is keenly unique. I've watched her grow from infancy, adulthood and now she is a gifted teacher and preacher. My perspective is that of the eldest brother and watching her mature over the years has been inspiring.

This book, **The 3:16 Challenge,** serves as a reminder that study is critical for our spiritual growth and development. Danielle has presented a Bible study that examines the 3:16 verses throughout the Bible, yes from Genesis to Revelation.

That is a distinct point of view for Bible study but certainly one that can be appreciated. Danielle's format is instructive and encouraging. As the study progresses, she solicits your attention to the verses being studied by connecting with the student to reflect on how this applies to their life. One such example is at the end of the Leviticus verse where she asks, "Does the term offering only resonate as a monetary term for you?"

The 3:16 Challenge has been an intriguing look at very specific verses that has captivated my study and encouraged me to continue growing leading to a deeper understanding of the Scriptures.

I am grateful for the opportunity to be a part of such a cutting-edge Bible Study.

Reverend Dante L. Rome
Pastor, St. James AME Church
Macon, Georgia
January 18, 2021

Table of Contents

The Baptism of Jesus..1

    Matthew 3:16

Name Change 7

    Mark 3:16

The Forerunner of Christ 13

    Luke 3:16

God's Love for Man 24

    John 3:16

Peter's Rebuke..37

    Acts 3:16

The Penalties of Sin...48

    Romans 3:16

Self Knowledge 57

    I Corinthians 3:16

Taking Away the Vail 65

    II Corinthians 3:16

The Promise to the Seed 71

    Galatians3:16

Strength to the Inner Man..80

    Ephesians 3:16

Let Us Mind the Same Thing 87

    Philippians 3:16

Let the Word of Christ Dwell in You Richly 93

    Colossians 3:16

The Lord of Peace 100

    II Thessalonians 3:16

The Mystery of Godliness 106

    I Timothy 3:16

All Scripture 116

    II Timothy 3:16

The Provocation 121

    Hebrews 3:16

Envying and Strife 126

    James 3:16

A Good Conscience 131

    I Peter 3:16

Know What You Know 137

    II Peter 3:16

Perceive We the Love of God 141

    I John 3:16

Lukewarm 144

    Revelation 3:16

Volume Two Reflection 152

WORKS CITED with Notes 153

Volume Two

New Testament 3:16 Challenge
Knowing Yourself through Relationship with God

The Baptism of Jesus

Matthew 3:16

Matthew 3:16 And Jesus, when he was baptized, went up straightway out of the water: and, lo, the heavens were opened unto him, and he saw the Spirit of God descending like a dove, and lighting upon him:

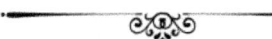

The Importance of Lineage

It can be argued that even today bloodline is very important - it does matter. In many places it matters more who you were born from than who you are currently becoming. The gospel writer Matthew was keenly aware of how much lineage mattered in his day; he took great pains to clearly establish the lineage of Christ right at the outset. But why? Because the Messiah had been prophesied for hundreds of years and people were desperate for his arrival. What is most curious is that when the Messiah was in their midst, walking in their very presence, he was somehow unrecognizable to them. Even with the prophecies on their lips, and ringing in their ears, their immediate situation blinded them to the Messiah in their midst. Their very history confirmed this truth and yet they refused to accept him.

Matthew 1:17 Thus there were fourteen generations in all from Abraham to David, fourteen from David to the exile to Babylon, and fourteen from the exile to Christ. [NIV]

Matthew does a great job of tracing the lineage from Abraham to David and from Baylon, and from Babylon to Christ himself but to some Jesus still was not the fulfillment of scripture. He was not who they were looking for because their circumstances, at least in their minds, called for someone else. So, in an effort to further validate this Jesus as the one identified in the Old Testament prophecies he goes on to describe the virgin birth of Christ. We meet Joseph, the espoused husband of Mary, the man who was to be the earthly father of Jesus. He was a man of integrity whose lineage could be traced through King David. As a man of integrity he had not touched his espoused wife and when she was found to be pregnant he did not want to disgrace her. "Because Joseph, her husband, was a righteous man and did not want to expose her to public disgrace, he had in mind to divorce her quietly" (Matt 1:19, NIV). What a man of integrity! He could have had her stoned but he chose instead to keep the situation quiet until God himself intervened in the person of an angel.

Matthew 1:20 But after he had considered this, an angel of the Lord appeared to him in a dream and said, "Joseph son of David, do not be afraid to take Mary home as your wife, because what is conceived in her is from the Holy Spirit.

Matthew 1:21 She will give birth to a son, and you are to give him the name Jesus, because he will save his people from their sins.

Matthew 1:22 And this took place to fulfill what the Lord had said through the prophet:

Matthew 1:23 "The virgin will be with child and will give birth to a son, they will call him Immanuel" - which means, "God with us."

And Joseph did as the angel of the Lord instructed him and Matthew is careful to add, just in case it be said that Mary was not virgin and that Joseph was his biological father, that they were not intimate until after the virgin birth had come to pass.

Matthew 1:24 When Joseph woke up, he did what the angel of the Lord had commanded him and took Mary home as his wife.

Matthew 1:25 But he had no union with her until she gave birth to a son.

And he gave him the name Jesus.

Now there could be no disputations as to the validity of the Christ. His identity was fully established by prophecy, history, and lineage. Surely this account would satisfy the Jewish audience to whom Matthew was directing his writings.

Chapter 2 further established the prophetic accounts of where the Messiah should be born and brings in the historical record of the Magi inquiring of Herod the Great where they could find the Messiah to worship him. The prophecy was confirmed for Herod and can be found in Micah 5:2 *But you, Bethlehem Ephrathah, though you are small among the clans[a] of Judah, out of you will come for me one who will be ruler over Israel, whose origins are from old, from ancient times"* (NIV). And we are familiar with the story, how Herod tried in vain to persuade them to give him all the specifics of where the infant Christ was and how they, after presenting gifts to the infant, were warned in a dream and went back another way. And likewise Joseph was warned in a dream to go to Egypt to preserve the life of the infant Jesus.

Matthew 2: 14 So he got up, took the child and his mother during the night and left for Egypt,
Matthew 2:15 where they stayed until the death of Herod. And so fulfilled what the Lord had said through the prophet: "Out of Egypt I called my son."

This event then brought about the horrific vengeance of Herod, the slaughter of the baby boys two years and under. Even though Herod knew he had been outsmarted by the Magi he still attempted to destroy the Messiah, thinking he could somehow circumvent that which had been prophesied. But I am so glad that no one has the power to circumvent the plans that God has ordained for our lives - not back in antiquity or now.

The fulfillment of prophecy continues as we encounter John the Baptist, the forerunner of Christ, preaching in the wilderness. He preached with boldness a message which is still relevant today, "Repent, for the kingdom of heaven is near" (Matthew 3:2, NIV). That is a timeless message for humanity to say the least. He was a bold preacher who did not bite his tongue. When the religious leaders of his day came to "see what he was doing" he called them out for their misguided leadership of God's people.

Matthew 3:7 But when he saw many of the Pharisees and Sadducees coming to where he was baptizing, he said to them: "You brood of vipers!" Who warned you to flee from the coming wrath?"

If only we were so bold in the face of unrighteousness in this generation! We too could root out the evil and sinfulness in our midst. Oh for the spirit and boldness of John the Baptist! And for all his boldness and the power of his ministry he was humble and submissive.

Matthew 3:13 Then Jesus came from Galilee to the Jordan to be baptized by John.
Matthew 3:14 But John tried to deter him, saying, "I need to be baptized by you, and do you come to me?"
Matthew 3:15 Jesus replied, "Let it be so now; it is proper for us to do this to fulfill all righteousness." Then John consented.

In the person of John the Baptist we learn the humility that is required for servantho by de by deod and ministry. Upon close examination of this first interaction between Jesus and John we see **humility and submission from both of them - these two cousins who changed the very world for all eternity - they are our teachers still on how to humble ourselves before our Holy God. Both of them had a calling on their lives and those callings intersected at the Jordan River.** And John was absolutely correct, the shoe could have been on the other foot. The Son of God was standing before him, waiting to be baptized, not out of the need for repentance but out of **obedience to God and in fulfillment of the divine plan for both their lives and ours as well.**

Matthew 3:16 As soon as Jesus was baptized, he went up out of the water. At that moment heaven was opened, and he saw the Spirit of God descending like a dove and lighting on him.
Matthew 3:17 And a voice from heaven said, "This is my Son, whom I love; with him I am well pleased."

What an awesome testimony from an act of humility and obedience! God himself responded to this action by Jesus and affirmed, out of his own mouth, exactly who Jesus is. **God called Jesus his son! Undeniable confirmation of the deity of our Lord. Irrefutable evidence that God is pleased with obedience - He was "Well Pleased!" God that this will be our testimony - that you speak these words concerning us. Unmistakable validation of that divine relationship - God calls Jesus his SON.** This is the **foundation of the confession of our faith in Christ - that he is the Son of the living God.** This is the basis of our Christian walk - Humble submission before our holy God. This is the aim of our earthly calling to ministry - That all we do be found pleasing in the sight of God. This is why we seek God so diligently - That we can revel in our **relationship** with our Heavenly Father! Amen, Amen, Amen.

Reflection

How has the establishment of the person and deity of Christ, in this gospel as recorded by Matthew, enlivened your faith?

_____

_____

_____

_____

_____

_____

_____

_____

_____

_____

_____

_____

Name Change

Mark 3:16

Mark 3:16 And Simon he surnamed Peter.

The Prophetic Beginnings

As we read through the writings of the gospel writers it becomes very clear that the targeted audience dictates the perspective of the writer. Matthew, writing to a Jewish audience,clearly takes on the perspective of the persuasive writer in an effort to convince his Jewish audience that JESUS was the prophesied Messiah. Mark, on the other hand, does not spend the opening verses establishing lineage at all. He seeks to establish Christ as the one sent by God to accomplish his will on the earth. This divine will was accomplished first through the mouth and hands of his forerunner, John the Baptist.

Mark 1:7 And this was his message: "After me will come one more powerful than I, the thongs of whose sandals I am not worthy to stoop down and untie.

Mark 1:8 I baptize you with water, but he will baptize you with the Holy Spirit.

Mark 1:9 At that time Jesus came from Nazareth in Galilee and was baptized by John in the Jordan.

Jesus is prophesied, has a forerunner, is obedient, and begins his public ministry with humble submission to the will of his Father. This is extremely important in establishing the character of Christ. We must see him distinctly as the one foretold by the prophets. We must see him as the Son of God. we must see him as both humble and obedient. **From the very beginning of Mark's gospel this is Jesus: prophesied, divine, humble, and obedient.** Once God acknowledges these truths we next see Jesus being led by the Spirit into the wilderness to be tempted by Satan for forty days. Talk about drama...from obedience to temptation but isn't that exactly how it goes?

We go from those brilliant moments of faith and obedience to the maelstrom of temptation. So what do you do when temptation comes your way? Know that our faith walk will be filled with many dangers but there is always help for us just as there was for Jesus. "And he was in the desert forty days, being tempted by Satan. He was with the wild animals, and angels attended him" (Mark 1:13). After this challenging time, Christ begins his public ministry. You have to know right here that after you weather your roughest storms, those times of preparation, then you'll be ready for the work that has been preordained for your hands. As this chapter comes to a close, Jesus is choosing his disciples because he needed them to come along so that they could be prepared for their ministry. He calls Simon and Andrew, James and John - all fishermen. They knew how to cast wide nets and catch fish - now it was time for them to learn how to catch men for the Messiah. They dropped their normal life and picked up this new life of ministry with Christ.

Mark 1:21 They went to Capernaum, and when the Sabbath came, Jesus went into the synagogue and began to teach.

Mark 1:22 The people were amazed at his teaching, because he taught them as one who had authority, not as the teachers of the law.

Mark 1:23 Just then a man in their synagogue who was possessed by an evil spirit cried out,

Mark 1:24 "What do you want with us, Jesus of Nazareth? Have you come to destroy us? I know who you are - the Holy One of God!"

Mark 1:25 "Be quiet!" said Jesus sternly. "Come out of him!"

Mark 1:26 The evil spirit shook the man violently and came out of him with a shriek.

Mark 1:27 The people were all so amazed that they asked each other, "What is this? A new teaching - and with authority! He even gives orders to evil spirits and they obey him."

Mark 1:28 News about him spread quickly over the whole region of Galilee.

From the initial moments of his public ministry Jesus demonstrated that he was different. He moved in his authority and men and demons responded. What power! He gave us the power to do the same and even greater works on the earth. He was not consumed with the fame that was following him, he remained humble and focused on his ministry. He even took the time to focus himself by getting by himself to pray. With that time of prayer taken for himself he was strengthened for the work and went forth preaching, teaching, and healing the sick.

So powerful was his public ministry that crowds followed them wherever they went. It was nearly impossible for some to get close to him but that did not deter them.

Mark 2:3 Some men came, bringing to him a paralytic, carried by four of them.

Mark 2:4 Since they could not get him to Jesus because of the crowd, they made an opening in the roof above Jesus and after digging through it, lowered the mat the paralyzed man was lying on.

Mark 2:5 When Jesus saw their faith, he said to the paralytic, "Son, your sins are forgiven you."

How amazing! Jesus responded not to the faith of the paralyzed man but to the faith of his friends. They knew that if they could just get their friend to where Jesus was that there was a blessing in store for their friend. My Lord, that we would all have friends with literal breakthrough faith! This is still the power of the ministry of Jesus - just seek him diligently, pursue him relentlessly, tear down what you need to tear down to get in his presence and watch him bless you! Jesus came to minister to all who needed to be ministered to. That is also still true today. His words can reach you right where you are! When the religious leaders of his day, the Pharisees, asked him about eating at Levi's house with lax collectors and sinners just look at his response from Mark 2:17, "On hearing this, Jesus said to them, "It is not the healthy who need a doctor, but the sick. I have not come to call the righteous, but sinners." He could not be dissuaded from his calling by any means. He then began to teach using parables to illuminate heavenly principles using earthly examples. He taught the people that legalism and righteousness were not one in the same.

The religious leaders of his era, similar to many today, sought to set themselves above the people by their appearance of holiness. What they had established was an impossible set of stifling rules which constantly separated them from God by their standards. These things, legalism and ritualism, were their own creations which they esteemed and which were irrelevant to the relationships that Christ came to welcome us all into. Therefore Jesus posed a very real threat to their institutionalized religious machine. Their manipulation of godly principles and ideals was disgusting in the eyes of God and Jesus came to present a true relationship with God and to demonstrate true holiness. They often disputed with him on points of the Law, issues with the Sabbath, the truth of God's kingdom, and prophecies concerning himself. They were determined to bring about the destruction of his ministry yet it continues to forth in this present age.

Christ continued to teach, preach, and heal as chapter 3 begins. He gives specific instructions to his disciples as to how to deal with the crowds that were coming to be taught and seeking healing. Then, from among the disciples, he calls the twelve.

Mark 3:13 Jesus went up on a mountainside and called to him those he wanted, and they came to him.

Mark 3:14 He appointed twelve - designating them apostles - that they might be with him and that he might send them out to preach.

Mark 3:15 and to have authority to drive out demons.

Mark 3:16 These are the twelve he appointed: Simon (to whom he gave the name Peter);

Mark 3:17 James son of Zebedee and his brother John (to them he gave the name Boanerges, which means Sons of Thunder);

Mark 3:18 Andrew, Philip, Bartholomew, Matthew, Thomas, James son of Alphaeus, Thaddeus, Simon the Zealot

Mark 3:19 and Judas Iscariot, who betrayed him.

Isn't it amazing to know that Jesus hand picks those he wants to do specific tasks? To think, Jesus called you and only you to do the things you are uniquely called to do. And more to the point he has a name that suits you perfectly! Not only did he come to earth to do something just for us but he has plans that are only for you - no one else can do it - only you. My Lord, how blessed we are!

Reflection

With what you've learned about Christ in this chapter, how do you know that Christ has moved uniquely in your life?

_____

_____

_____

_____

_____

_____

_____

_____

_____

_____

_____

_____

The Forerunner of Christ

Luke 3:16

Luke 3:16 John answered, saying unto them all, I indeed baptize you with water; but one mightier than I cometh, the latchet of whose shoes I am not worthy to unloose: he shall baptize you with the Holy Ghost and with fire:

An Answer to Prayer

As Luke opens his gospel account, he begins with the introduction that explains more clearly to Theophilus the things which he has been taught about Christ and his forerunner John. He affirms the priesthood and faithful prayers of Zacharias and the barrenness of his wife Elisabeth. Why is that significant? The word teaches us that they were both "...now well stricken in years" (Luke 1:7). That should have, at least in the minds of many, negated God's affirmation of the prayer requests for a son. They had become old together and were still childless. However, even with their prayer apparently having been answered with a "NO" Zacharias continued to faithfully serve in his capacity to the LORD.

Luke 1:8 And it came to pass, that while he executed the priest's office before God in the order of his course,

Luke 1:9 According to this custom of the priest's office, his lot was to burn incense when he went into the temple of the Lord.

Luke 1:10 And the whole multitude of the people were praying without at the time of incense.

Luke 1: 11 And there appeared unto him an angel of the Lord standing on the right side of the altar of incense.

Luke 1: 12 And when Zacharias saw him, he was troubled, and fear fell upon him.

Luke 1:13 But the angel said unto him, Fear not, Zacharias: for thy prayer is heard; and thy wife Elisabeth shall bear thee a son, and thou shalt call his name John.

What strikes me in these verses are these things:

- Even though his prayer request had seemingly been denied, Zacharias continued to be faithful to his calling and servanthood to the Lord.

- I noticed the unity of the people - all praying together and in their appropriate position.

- What did I glean from those things? As we saw God is moved by faithful obedience.

- Prayers prayed in faith are answered...even if it takes years of pressing in and trusting God.

Faithful obedience led to an unexpected encounter with an angelic being, sent from God, who both affirmed that those long prayed prayers had been heard and that the answer was the long awaited "YES" he had prayed for. Yet I know discouragement, disobedience, and disregard are often our response to what we perceive to be unanswered prayers. What am I saying?

When God does not move in our timing we are too often so discouraged that we almost forget how to pray or cease to pray altogether. The "rejection" of our request is too much for us and out of a pure pout, that's right - a pout, we are discouraged and do damage to our prayer relationship to our Holy God. Or we become disobedient and fail to execute those things which have been ordained for our hands and appointed to us for our completion. Or we flatly disregard our proper position of humility before God, who is afterall, omniscient and knows, better than we do, what we are equipped to handle. Yes, those long prayed prayers can be extremely hard for some of us but the example and truth of the lives of Zachariah and Elisabeth prove that we must continue to press on and we will see the glory of God.

Then the angel goes on to tell Zacharias who his son will be, establishing his calling and anointing that will be manifested even from the time his mother carries him in her womb. This is no ordinary child - God has a need for him to prepare His people for their coming Messiah. Yet, knowing what he had prayed for, he still had a crucial moment of doubt.

Luke 1:18 And Zacharias said unto the angel, Whereby shall I know this?
For I am an old man, and my wife is well stricken in years.
Luke 1:19 And the angel answering said unto him, I am Gabriel, that stand in the presence of God; and am sent to speak unto thee, and to shew thee these glad tidings.
Luke 1:20 And, behold, thou shalt be dumb, and not able to speak, until the day that these things shall be performed, because thou believest not my words, which shall be fulfilled in their season.

And we read on to find that Zacharias is truly mute and that he served his appointed time in the temple then went home to his wife. And she conceived. Then Gabriel, that same angelic being, visited Mary to tell her that she would also bear a son. And the virgin asked a similar question of Gabriel, "How shall this be, seeing I know not a man?" (Luke 1:34) Now I wondered why she did not have a similar fate to that of Zacharias for asking essentially the same question. Here's what was revealed to me:

- Zacharias question came from the position of doubt - This something he had been praying for and had expected. It had taken so long in coming that it had become impossible in his mind because of the frailty he perceived in himself and his wife.

- Mary's question came from a place of sincere confusion. She knew herself to be a virgin and she misunderstood the means by which this immaculate conception would be done in her. She needed clarification - she was not in doubt.

Luke 1:35 And the angel answered and said unto her, The Holy Ghost shall come upon thee, and the power of the Highest shall overpower thee: therefore also that holy thing which shall be born of thee shall be called the Son of God.

Luke 1:36 And, behold, thy cousin Elisabeth, she hath also conceived a son in her old age: and this is the sixth month with her, who was called barren.

Luke 1:37 For with God nothing shall be impossible.

Luke 1:38 And Mary said, Behold the handmaid of the Lord: be it unto me according to thy word, And the angel departed from her.

This first chapter of Luke is 80 verses of some of the richest testimonies of the power of obedience and faith in the lives of believers. We find that the word that was spoken of Elisabeth came to pass and she delivered her son. On the eighth day, in keeping with tradition, the infant was to be circumcised and named. Now the name was known to Zacharias and to Elisabeth but no one else. Tradition would have dictated that this long awaited son be named after his father and be called Zacharias - yet the angel Gabriel had decreed otherwise. Sometimes tradition is so strong in our lives that it would lead us to disobedience.

Luke 1:59 And it came to pass, that on the eighth day they came to circumcise the child; and they called him Zacharias, after the name of his father.

Luke 1:60 And his mother answered and said, Not so; but he shall be called John.

Luke 1:61 And they said unto her, There is none of thy kindred that is called by this name.

Luke 1:62 And they made signs to his father, how he would have him called.

Luke 1:63 And he asked for a writing table, and wrote, saying, His name is John. And they marvelled all.

Luke 1:64 And his mouth was opened immediately, and his tongue loosed, and he spake, and praised God.

Luke 1:65 And fear came on all that dwelt round about them: and all these sayings were noised abroad throughout all the hill country of Judea.

Luke 1:66 And all they that heard them laid them up in their hearts, saying What manner of child shall this be! And the hand of the Lord was with him.

From Luke chapter 1 we learn that the promises of God are well worth waiting for. Luke chapter 2 opens with that taxation that had been called for under Caesar Augustus and which led Joseph and Mary to the City of David, Bethlehem. The prophesied birth of the Messiah is going to come to pass. This faith event meets up with history to validate for us, in this present age, that this word is true. The bible records that the decree was sent down from Caesar Augustus and first made by Cyrenius. It was during this trip to fulfill their civic responsibilities that Christ was born.

Luke 2:4 And Joseph also went up from Galilee, out of the city of Nazareth, into Judaea, unto the city of David, which is called Bethlehem; (because he was of the house and lineage of David:)
Luke 2:5 To be taxed with Mary, his espoused wife, being great with child. Luke 2:6 And so it was, that, while they were there, the days were accomplished that she should be delivered.
Luke 2:7 And she brought forth her first-born son, and wrapped him in swaddling clothes, and laid him in a manger; because there was no room for them in the inn.

We are further presented with the reality that timing, God's timing, is essential as Mary and Joseph fulfill the traditions of circumcision on the eighth day after the birth of a male child, during which time a sacrifice is made at the time of presentation to the Lord. Then we meet Simeon, one who had literally waited his entire life to see the prophesied Christ. This wait was likely a decades long wait and in all that time Simeon was assured of the fact that he would live to see this prophecy come to pass. And for many of us a mere day is too long to wait on the fulfillment of the promises of the Lord in our lives.

Luke 2:25 And, behold, there was a man in Jerusalem, whose name was Simeon; and the same man was just and devout, waiting for the consolation of Israel: and the Holy Ghost was upon him.
Luke 2:26 And it was revealed unto him by the Holy Ghost, that he should not see death, before he had seen the Lord's Christ.

What is it that God has spoken unto you? Has it been long coming in your estimation? Do not fool yourself - our understanding of time is not in alignment with

God's. What seems unreasonably long to us could well be a time of preparation for us. Whatever the reason God truly knows best. So Simeon had waited and it came to pass in his lifetime as it had been promised. In this same chapter, just a few more verses on, we learn of the faith of the prophetess Anna. How she has served in the temple by fasting and praying for years. Even after the grief of losing her husband years earlier she continued to serve.

Luke 2:37 And she was a widow of about fourscore and four years, which departed not from the temple, but served God with fastings and prayers night and day.

Luke 2:38 And she coming in that instant gave thanks likewise unto the Lord and spake of him to all them that looked for redemption in Jerusalem.

Not only did she serve faithfully but she bore witness to the reality that salvation had come to God's people. Yes, it had taken generations yet she could proclaim it boldly - the promise had come!

The accounts that are recorded here provide a glimpse into the lives of Joseph, Mary, and those who were going about their lives with the expectation that God would fulfill His promises. All these events had been prophesied of old and to some degree were very clear expectations in the timing of God. However, even in the lives of the chosen, the unexpected can come to pass and so it does in the events recorded in Luke 2:41-52. We have an instance here of people doing what is right in the sight of the Lord and then sheer terror strikes at their hearts. In the midst of their return journey to Jerusalem, an annual pilgrimage for devout Jews, the worst thing that could happen to parents occurs - they realize their child is missing.

Luke 2:41 Now his parents went to Jerusalem every year at the feast of the passover.

Luke 2:42 And when he was twelve years old, they went up to Jerusalem after the custom of the feast.

Luke 2:43 And when they had fulfilled the days, as they returned, the child Jesus tarried behind in Jerusalem; and Joseph and his mother knew not of it.

Luke 2:44 But they, supposing him to have been in the company, went a day's journey; and they sought him among their kinsfolk and acquaintances.

Luke 2:45 And when they found him not, they turned back again to Jerusalem, seeking him.

Luke 2:46 And it came to pass, that after three days they found him in the temple, sitting in the midst of the doctors, both hearing them, and asking them questions.

Luke 2:47 And all that heard him were astonished at his understanding and answers.

I can only imagine the flood of emotion that those four days had brought to his parents. Four days of not knowing where he was while knowing who he was. The terror, guilt, second guessing of their own actions had to have been devastating. Here it is God has entrusted the rearing of his son into the hands of earthly parents and...you lost him. How to explain that to God. Yet they persevered until they found him, in the very place they had been, Jerusalem in the Temple. Seems obvious that that is where he would have been because he was coming of age and was beginning to understand, because he was afterall a flesh and blood child, who he was. The fact that his parents were devout to their faith, making the annual pilgrimage, is honorable. They were instilling in their human child Jesus a love for the things of His heavenly Father. We cannot not assume that his divinity was awakened in him at this point. He was fully human while simultaneously being fully divine; he was a human child who needed the nurture, love, and instruction that all human children need though not all receive. What a daunting calling - raising Christ!

As a parent I have gone through the uncertainties that are part and parcel of having children. I know that our daughters are gifts from God. I was told that, after one healthy pregnancy and one tragic miscarriage, I would not be able to maintain a pregnancy ever again. That's what man said but God had other plans for us and our family. He gifted us with two more daughters, 19 months apart from each other, who are uniquely gifted, as they all have been. I know that all of our daughters are special and that we haven't been perfect parents. But I know God entrusted them to my husband and I to raise in the reverence and knowledge of Him. That is the greatest calling of our lives. Yet our reality does not compare to the divine nature of the calling to parent Jesus. My heart skips a beat when I read these passages...I don't want to ever know the terror of not knowing where our children are for an hour let alone four days. The panic must have been real every step back to Jerusalem. My Lord they must have prayed every step of the search until they heard his voice and laid eyes on him in the Temple. But the relief, which quickly turned to the parental chastisement, when they knew he was fine.

Luke 2:48 And when they saw him, they were amazed: and his mother said unto him, Son, why hast thou thus dealt with us? Behold, thy father and I have sought thee sorrowing.

That strikes to the heart of parental love. Why would you do this? How could you do this to us? It's a question that speaks to fears and beliefs. After four days they had probably begun to believe he had been killed. After four days the Jewish custom was to believe that death was permanent, no hope of coming back to the land of the living. They thought the worst. This mother's question was so very sincere. Why would you deal with us like this? Why make us believe you are gone forever? Her heart was grieving, they were hurt. But then the child Jesus responds in a way that clearly demonstrates he is beginning to understand who he is.

Luke 2:49 And he said unto them, How is it that ye sought me? Wist ye not that I must be about my Father's business?
Luke 2:50 And they understood not the saying which he spake unto them. Luke 2:51 And he went down with them, and came to Nazareth, and was subject unto them: but his mother kept all these sayings in her heart. Luke 2:52 And Jesus increased in wisdom and stature, and in favour with God and man.

In those moments, when Jesus is offering an answer to his mother's question she is looking only at her human child. She does not comprehend that he understands or at least has begun to understand who he is. That is the same limiting perspective many still have of Jesus today. We are comfortable seeing the humanity of Jesus but we are likewise confused by the divinity of Jesus. Why is this true? Easy - we understand humanity. We get the realities, limitations, and capabilities of our humanity. Our divine connections - our spirit man, we grapple with as we breathe each breath. We are still mystified by all that Jesus is, just like his mother was. And similarly, like his mother, we get to know more about him as we endeavor to know him. He realized this truth and was **subject** to them.

Subject [5293] hupotasso in the Greek, means *to be under obedience* as defined in the Strong's Exhaustive Concordance. And we do not hear of him straying away from them again - he honored his earthly parents. We learn that Jesus grew in **wisdom [4678] sophia,** (higher or lower, worldly or spiritual) wisdom; **stature [2244] helikia,** maturity (in years or size); **favour [5485] charis,** gracious of manner or act; the divine influence upon the heart, and its reflection in life; Jesus was growing into the calling for his earthly ministry. Luke introduces us to the political and religious atmosphere in chapter 3.

Roman rule was well established in the region and their rule was absolute. The religious establishment of Judaea sought more the loyalties of the people than the growth of sincere worship. And it is into this environment John bursts forth as a voice crying in the wilderness.

Luke 3:1 Now in the fifteenth year of the reign of Tiberius Caesar, Pontius Pilate being governor of Judaea, and Herod being tetrarch of Galilee, and his brother Philip tetrarch of Ituraea and of the region of Trachonitis, and

Lysanias the tetrarch of Abilene,

Luke 3:2 Annas and Caiaphas he came into all the country about Jordan, preaching the baptism of repentance for the remission of sins;

John was beginning his ministry in the wilderness as it had been prophesied. His message was extremely straightforward - "repent for the remission of sins". His message alluded to the reality that calling on the connection to Abraham for the promise of salvation would not be enough.

Luke 3:8 Bring forth therefore fruits worthy of repentance, and begin not to say within yourselves, We have Abraham to our father: for I say unto you, That God is able of these stones to raise up children unto Abraham.

That is an important pronouncement even today as many people claim that relationship to those who are true faithful worshippers is enough to gain your salvation. Let me assure you that salvation must be sought on a personal level. Confession of belief is personal. The walk of faith is personal. Your eternal reality - yes - is personal. We do well to do what those who came to John did - they asked the pivotal question found in Luke 3:10, "..."What shall we do then?" John then gives a litany of answers specific to situations.

His responses in Luke 3:11-14 come down to share your blessings and treat people as you should. Sounds quite familiar and for so many these things are unbelievably troublesome. They call for self examination and action. Self sacrifice and righteous living don't seem hard but for some these philosophies put them at odds with the societal norm and personal lifestyle. That is still true today and is a challenge for more people than we can even imagine or would like to believe. The same reaction would likely occur - we wonder how it would even be possible to live that kind of life - a life so closely aligned to godliness. Yet we know, like they did, that this life in Christ requires something of us. The forerunner told them and speaks to us now with the answer.

Luke 3:16 John answered, saying unto them all, I indeed baptize you with water; but one mightier than I cometh, the latchet of whose shoes I am not worthy to unloose: he shall baptize you with the Holy Ghost and with fire.

This same Mighty One is available to us to baptize with the gift of the Holy Spirit - the one who comforts and intercedes, or guides us and with fire that purges and purifies. My Lord, what a word of hope and truth John ministered. His ministry still speaks the truth of Jesus Christ and we await his return.

Reflection

What lessons have you gleaned from these early chapters in Luke?

_____

_____

_____

_____

_____

_____

How can these be applied meaningfully to your life?

_____

_____

_____

_____

_____

_____

God's Love for Man

John 3:16

John 3:16 For God so loved the world, that he gave his only begotten Son, that whosoever believeth in him should not perish, but have everlasting life.

IN THE BEGINNING

John opens his gospel with awe inspiring revelations about the WORD - it always existed. It existed with God, and in fact was God. Talk about establishing what really matters first - the preeminence of the Word and God and simultaneously asserting that they are one in the same. Let's just take that in for a moment...the Word, that always was, is God. Now we understand the triune nature of God, the reality that He is three distinct beings in one - Father, Son, and Holy Spirit. And this assertion confirms that the second person of the Trinity, the Son, was with God in the form of the Word and that the Word is God just as the Son is God. He is the creator of all that is. Life is in him; light is in him. He is the light that shines in darkness and is incomprehensible. All this is revealed in the first five verses.

Then we are told of his forerunner, John, and his purpose. "The same came for a witness, to bear witness of the Light, that all men through him might believe" (John 1:7). And his purpose was great, to prepare all who would receive the Word for it. His calling was a great one but he was very clear on who he was and also of his purpose. He was awaiting the coming Messiah and when the time arrived he fulfilled his purpose.

24

John 1:15 John bare witness of him, and cried, saying, This was he of whom I spake, He that cometh after me is preferred before me: for he was before me.

John 1:16 And of his fulness have all we received, and grace for grace.

John 1:17 For the law was given by Moses, but grace and truth came by Jesus Christ.

That was the message that John preached and he was quite explicitly clear yet he was questioned by the religious leaders of his day. It was as if they were trying to catch him in some sinister lie, as if he was part of some plot to deceive the world. He remained consistent because he was absolutely clear in his role - forerunner of Christ.

John 1:19 And this is the record of John, when the Jews sent priests and Levites from Jerusalem to ask him, Who art thou?

John 1:20 And he confessed, and denied not; but confessed, I am not the Christ.

John 1:21 And they asked him, What then? Art thou Elias? And he saith, I am not. Art thou a prophet? And he answered, No.

John 1:22 Then said they unto him, Who art thou? That we may give an answer to them that sent us. What sayest thou of thyself?

John 1:23 He said, I Am THE VOICE OF ONE CRYING IN THE WILDERNESS, MAKE STRAIGHT THE WAY OF THE LORD, as said the prophet Esaias.

The religious leaders thought that they might have worn him down, making him change his story, but he said the same thing each time. If only we could stick to the story of who God has said we are with that kind of tenacity we would avoid much of the agony of this life. The knowledge of this supreme truth, who we are in Christ, is both revelatory and transformative. This word of truth from God is freedom while also being servitude. This word of truth immediately stirs us while eternally steering. Some many dichotomies - all true. The Pharisees continued to engage John the Baptist and he continues to affirm who Christ is and his purpose, even referring to Jesus in verse 29 as "the Lamb of God, which taketh away the sin of the world." Then he takes on a very interesting perspective - one in which he himself has not known Jesus. The kind of knowledge that he is referring to is a clarity of understanding, an almost intimacy of knowing on an extremely deep level - not a trivial understanding but personally and unwaveringly - that type of knowledge had escaped him when it came to Jesus until the day of his baptism.

John 1:32 And John bare record, saying, I saw the Spirit descending from heaven like a dove, and it abode upon him.

John 1:33 And I knew him not: but he that sent me to baptize with water, the same said unto me, Upon whom thou shalt see the Spirit descending, and remaining on him, the same is he which baptizeth with the Holy Ghost.

John 1:34 And I saw, and bare record that this is the Son of God.

In the days which followed John the Baptist again affirms Jesus as the Lamb of God and two of his disciples began to follow Jesus, becoming his first disciples.

John 1:40 One of the two which heard John speak, and followed him, was Andrew, Simon Peter's brother.

John 1:41 He first findeth his own brother, Simon, and saith unto him, We have found the Messias, which is being interpreted, the Christ.

John 1:42 And he brought him to Jesus. And when Jesus beheld him, he said, Thou art Simon the son of Jona: thou shalt be called Cephas, which is by interpretation, A stone.

And thus started the public ministry of Christ. With those two he began to teach and minister. Then came Philip and Nathanael, with whom he had an interesting exchange on the issue of belief and how Jesus had come to know him.

John 1:47 Jesus saw Nathanael coming to him, and saith of him, Behold an Israelite indeed, in whom is no guile!

John 1:48 Nathanael saith unto him, Whence knowest thou me? Jesus answered and said unto him, Before that Philip called thee, when thou wast under the fig tree, I saw thee.

The type of seeing that Jesus is referring to here is more than just the visual perception. It is the kind of seeing that provides perception and depth of knowledge - he saw exactly who Nathanael was. He saw him in a way that only the divine can see. He saw Nathanael in the same way he sees us - beyond what we can know about ourselves. He sees to the depths of spirit and soul, more than the outside, the depths of who we are. Passed attempts at perfection, beyond the scars of emotional pain, overlooking the past, and into our future - he sees us. Now Nathanael is impressed with the little that he understands of what Jesus has spoken to him but there is more.

John 1:49 Nathanael answered and saith unto him, Rabbi, thou art the Son of God; thou art the King of Israel.

John 1:50 Jesus answered and said unto him, Because I said unto thee, I saw thee under the fig tree, believest thou? Thou shalt see greater things than these.

John 1:51 And he saith unto him, Verily, verily, I say unto you, Hereafter ye shall see heaven open, and the angels of God ascending and descending upon the Son of man.

Now, from John 1:48-51 the words saw and see are used four times. That struck me as being significant so I looked a bit deeper to understand clearly what Jesus was saying to Nathanael. Strong's Exhaustive Concordance offers the following definitions of saw and see in this specific context.

Saw [1492] (eido) - to know, be aware; behold, consider, knowledge, perceive.

See [3700] (optanomai) - to gaze at with wide open eyes as at something remarkable What is Jesus saying here? He tells Nathanael, in essence, you were amazed because I saw who you actually are but that is truly nothing compared to what you will see. The "seeing" is more than the mechanical workings of vision. This kind of seeing elicits knowledge and wonder respectively. Jesus sees us and knows us. We see the divine and are struck with wonder and awe. And we are still struck by the magnificence of God, Jesus, and the Holy Spirit.

So now let's get some perspective on how rapidly this account is moving. Day one John the Baptist is being questioned by the pharisees. Day two disciples of John begin to follow Jesus and call him Rabbi. He tells them that there is so much more to learn and see. Day three, which begins chapter 2, is the wedding in Cana of Galilee. Jesus and his disciples are in attendance to this wedding along with Mary, his mother. Mary, being a true mother and not wanting the host of the feast to suffer embarrassment due to a lack of provisions for his guests, tells Jesus that there is a problem. It's not lost on me that she did not try to fix it first herself - she went directly to the one whom she knew had the power to fix it. Life lesson for us right there.

John 2:1 And the third day there was a marriage in Cana of Galilee; and the mother of Jesus was there:

John 2:2 And both Jesus was called, and his disciples, to the marriage.

John 2:3 And when they wanted wine, the mother of Jesus saith unto him, They have no wine.

John 2:4 Jesus saith unto her, Woman, what have I to do with thee? Mine hour is not yet come.

John 2:5 His mother saith unto the servants, Whatsoever he saith unto you, do it.

John 2:6 And there were set there six waterpots of stone, after the manner of the purifying of the Jews, containing two or three firkins apiece.

John 2:7 Jesus saith unto them, Fill the waterpots with water. And they filled them up to the brim.

John 2:8 And he saith unto them, Draw out now, and bear unto the governor of the feast. And they bear it.

John 2:9 When the ruler of the feast had tasted the water that was made wine, and knew not whence it was;(but the servants which drew the water knew;) the governor of the feast called the bridegroom,

John 2:10 And saith unto him, Every man at the beginning doth set forth good wine; and when men have well drunk, then that which is worse: but thou hast kept the good wine until now. John 2:11 This beginning of miracles did Jesus in Cana of Galilee, and manifested forth his glory; and his disciples believed on him.

What strikes you most powerfully about this first miracle of Jesus? Here's what strikes me:

- Mary sought Jesus for someone other than herself. INTERCESSION
- She made the request known to Jesus with boldness and went on. **EXPECTANCY**
- Jesus responded immediately and used what was there. IMMEDIACY

- Jesus also used the water that they used, though for a different purpose. INTENTIONALITY

- Jesus then told them to bring the wine to the one in charge of the gathering. CLARITY

This first miracle is amazing on so many levels. Mary didn't even ask something of Jesus for herself. Jesus's first miracle was performed as Mary interceded on behalf of someone else. What does that say about the power of intercession? Even the banter from Jesus did not shake her faith in his ability to step in and address the immediate need. I am moved by her selflessness and her boldness. The selflessness is obvious - she went to him for them - those who had organized the wedding feast. These wedding feasts went on for days and the more the family had to share with the community the better off the union of the couple was thought to be. How demoralizing it would have been to have it be remembered that you ran out of wine at your wedding feast! They would have been the talk of that community for years to come. Mary eliminated that culture stigma from them. How can I claim boldness?

Boldness is obvious as well because she didn't even acknowledge Jesus's response to her. Her next words were to the servants - "Whatever he saith unto you, do it". She knew the miraculous was about to unfold in their midst. She had known that the miraculous was in him from the time it was prophesied that she would bear the Son of God in her womb. Undoubtedly she knew this was the awaited moment for the world to begin to know who he was. Then the miraculous begins to unfold...

Waterpots used for purification should not have been the same ones used to bear wine for consumption. Yet those are the waterpots Jesus chose as the vessels for this first miracle. Why is this sticking out for me? It's unexpected. Those waterpots were used to hold the water used to make one clean, not to hold that which would refresh you. They were not the vessels that held that which would bring the esteem of guests at a celebration. These were the vessels that held that which purified from uncleanness; those waters were to restore right standing in the eyes of men. No, these vessels were not vessels of honor, yet Jesus used them for just that purpose. The servants did exactly what he said, filling the pots to the brim and then taking them to the governor of the feast.

We are not told that Jesus spoke a word over the pots, waved his hands over the pots, winked at the pots, none of that. So what brought about the miracle? OBE-DIENCE. Here's what else did not happen - The servants did not say "These aren't the wine containers…" They did what Mary said to do which was whatever Jeus said to do. They, without question, did what Jesus said. It must have seemed ridiculous but they did it. They must have wondered what would happen when they brought the sample to the governor of the feast - all they knew was that there was water in the vessel that they were bringing to him. Still they were obedient. They may have even thought to themselves "Why are we bringing this man this water?" but they still brought it. Could you or I have done that? Would we have had to have more information or at least clarity before going before this governor? Probably but the blessing was in their obedience. The miracle took place as they were walking to bring what they knew was water to a governor who expected wine. They brought what Jesus sent them with and were utterly astonished when they realized what they had. Isn't that what Jesus does though? He sends us, and in our minds we have one thing and in the midst of our going he has transformed what we carry into exactly what he intends to use for his glory! The shout goes right there!

And what exploits did Jesus do after the wedding feast at Cana? From there he, Mary, his brethren, and disciples went to Jerusalem for it was the time of the Passover. Jesus is quite literally about to begin to clean house.

John 2:13 And the Jews' passover was at hand, and Jesus went up to Jerusalem,

John 2:14 And found in the temple those that sold oxen and sheep and doves, and the changers of money sitting:

John 2:15 And when he had made a scourge of small cords, he drove them all out of the temple, and the sheep, and the oxen; and poured out the changers' money and overthrew the tables;

John 2:16 And said unto them that sold doves, Take these things hence; make not my Father's house an house of merchandise.

It is important here not to miss exactly why Jesus would have taken the time to make a scourge and cleanse the temple. BibleReference.com offers the following explanation:

The work of the livestock vendors and money changers probably started off with good intentions. Jews coming to the temple did not always have the means to bring animals with them. So, it made sense to provide a way to purchase proper sacrifices. There was also good reason to help people convert their coins into local money. Apparently, interest in making money soon took over. And, instead of conducting business near the temple, or just outside it, the marketplace had been moved inside the temple grounds.

The area in question is known as the "Court of the Gentiles," just inside the borders of the temple. This should have been the place where Israel reached out to tell others about God. Instead, it was being used as a blatant money grab. Part of the warning in this story is the danger in allowing a ministry to become a business, and losing sight of its original purpose. Worse, is the threat of letting business concerns outweigh spiritual concerns.

This was more than just Jesus displaying righteous indignation due to the scandalous financial abuses happening in the temple; it was about the blatant disregard for ministry to all who came there seeking to know God. Therefore he beat the money changers who were cheating the people who earnestly wanted to make sacrifices in the temple and he released the animals, oxen and sheep, these most costly animals needed for the blood sacrifices. I pondered that fact - why release these animals? I learned that the oxen was necessary for the harvest because it was the strongest animal that had been domesticated in that region. Without them the harvest would not be possible. The symbolism is extremely powerful. These jews were missing the harvest of humanity in their pursuit of financial gain. Not only were they missing an opportunity to bring gentiles to the living God but they were misleading God's chosen people who had so frequently been referred to as sheep in need of a shepherd. "Sheep are mentioned in the Bible more than 500 times, more than any other animal. The prominence of sheep in the Bible grows out of two realities. Sheep were important to the nomads and agricultural life of the Hebrews and similar peoples. Secondly, sheep are used throughout the Bible to symbolically refer to God's people" (sheep 101). However Jesus took the time to speak with those who sold doves.He tells them not to make "his Father's house a house of merchandise."

Jesus is giving a valid word of warning that speaks a truth across the millennium. The word for merchandise that he uses is emporion which should look familiar to us - it's where we get our word emporium which is essentially a shopping mall. He said to them don't make the place of worship a place of enterprise. Our goal in the Lord's house is not to sell anyone anything but rather to make the presentation of Christ. We're not sales people, we are ministers and servants. We too are very much in need of this reminder because "Selling the Gospel" has become very big business while ministry has taken a backseat. Sad but true but that reality must transform before the return of Christ. As chapter 2 comes to a close we hear Jesus saying to the Jews in John 2:19 "Destroy this temple, and in three days I will raise it up." But they misunderstood what he was saying, taking him literally about the temple in which they stood when he was in fact speaking of his own body. He was telling them to their faces exactly what would happen as he fulfilled the scripture concerning his own resurrection. Unfortunately, as John the Baptist had said again and again, they knew him not. Even though that was the case then, and for many even today, many believed him once they witnessed the miracles he performed in their midst. Chapter 3 opens with the interaction between Jesus and Nicodemus, a Pharisee.

Nicodemus is a very interesting fellow. He comes to Jesus on the downlow to tell him that they, presumably the other Pharisees, know exactly who he is. So the question begs to be asked "Why come to Jesus under the cover of night?" If this is common knowledge and acknowledged belief why the secrecy? I have had similar conversations with many people who secretly believe but are uncomfortable expressing their belief openly. You know, it wouldn't be a "good look" for them. That reality aside - they still have strong convictions about and burning questions for the Savior.

John 3:1 There was a man of the Pharisees, named Nicodemus, a ruler of the Jews: John 3:2 The same came to Jesus by night, and said unto him, Rabbi, we know thou art a teacher come from God: for no man can do these miracles that thou doest, exceptGod be with him.

John 3:3 Jesus answered and said unto him, Verily, verily, I say unto thee, Except a man be born again, he cannot see the kingdom of God.

John 3:4 Nicodemus saith unto him, How can a man be born when he is old? Can he enter the second time into his mother's womb, and be born?

John 3:5 Jesus answered, Verily, verily, I say unto the, Except a man be born of water and of the Spirit, he cannot enter into the kingdom of God.

John 3:6 That which is born of the flesh is flesh; and that which is born of the Spirit is spirit.

John 3:7 Marvel not that I said unto thee, Ye must be born again.

John 3:8 The wind bloweth where it listeth, and thou hearest the sound thereof, but canst not tell whence it cometh, and whither it goeth: so is every one that is born of the Spirit.

This conversation between Jesus and Nicodemus is so interesting because at the heart of it is the idea of rebirth and seeing the kingdom of God. The rebirth that Jesus is alluding to is not the physical action of coming forth from our mother's womb. On the other hand it is the idea of gennao, the Greek word which carries the notion of regeneration which means to make new. This, then, is not a physical renewal but wholly spiritual. As chapter 2 closes we see John writing that Jesus "knew all men" and that "he knew what was in man". Clearly a reference to the sinful nature that we struggle daily to overcome. We fail to understand how strong that nature is within us but there is another nature that is within us that we learn to tap into once we confess our belief in Christ and are born in the Spirit. This Spirit is the pneuma, the mental disposition, the rational soul, the vital principle, or the superhuman [angel, demon, or divine God], the Holy Spirit. Jesus is saying that there is much more to us than we understand and though it seems marvelous it is attainable. We are like the very wind - it is not known where it comes from yet there is evidence of it - that is who we are, those of us who are born of the Spirit. Nicodemus. Like most of us, was still perplexed by this conversation. I too have so many questions but I choose to walk in the acceptance of the fact that there are some things that I simply will not know until Jesus fully reveals all things on that day. Jesus goes into the legalistic language that we are coming to expert from the Jewish leaders.

John 3:11 Verily, verily, I say unto thee, We speak that we know, and testify that we have seen; and ye receive not our witness.
John 3:12 If I have told you earthly things, and ye believe not, how shall ye believe, if I tell you of heavenly things?

Here it is critical to realize the preexistent nature of Jesus. Before he took on human flesh he already existed in heaven. That being the case he is well qualified to speak authoritatively of those things which he experienced and witnessed in heaven. Therefore he gives his testimony that can be taken as the TRUTH. And he asks a pertinent question -If I have told you earthly things, and ye believe not, how shall ye believe, if I tell you of heavenly things? That is still a valid question - If he's told us the truth about the things we need to do on earth to have eternal life with him and we still have chosen not to believe then how can we possibly receive the mysteries that he has to reveal? Impossible right? And likely the reason why we continue to search the world and the heavens for a truth that is right before us. Then he goes on to reveal a series of truths.

John 3:13 And no man hath ascended up to heaven, but he that came down from heaven, even the Son of man which is in heaven.
John 3:14 And as Moses lifted up the serpent in the wilderness, even so must the Son of man must be lifted up:
John 3:15 That whosoever believeth in him should not perish, but have eternal life.

Jesus is establishing in the consciousness of men who exactly he is. He is the only one who has come down to earth from heaven - the only one. In his preexistent form it has already been established that he was the word that came to earth and dwelt among us. This is being established in the moments that he is talking with Nicodemus. He is the Holy One from heaven who is in their midst. Then he reminds them of another truth which they have no issue affirming - Moses lifting that serpent in the wilderness. What was the purpose of that event - They were told to look up and live. It was an acknowledgement of their sin and the looking up to a Holy God for forgiveness, reconciliation, and restoration. That is what will be required again as they will look on Jesus as he hangs on Calvary's cross. They will be required to look up again and live. We are likewise required to look to Christ in obedience, turn away from our sinful nature and actions, receiving forgiveness, reconciliation and restoration from the only one worthy to bestow those gifts upon us.

John 3:16 For God so loved the world, that he gave his only begotten Son, that whosoever believeth in him should not perish, but have everlasting life.

Now we have arrived at the verse for our entire endeavor in this book, so let's go deeper. I want you to see this scripture with fresh eyes. I want it to be elevated from the realm of cliche and have the depth of meaning that understanding the language of the day brings.

For God so agapao [to love in a social and moral sense] the world, that he didomi [delivered up] his only begotten Son, that whosoever pisteuo [entrusted their well-being especially to Christ] in him should not apollumi [be destroyed fully] but have everlasting zoe [life, lifetime].

Take it in with fresh eyes of gratitude and humility. This is what God did for us. As unworthy as we are and will continue to be - he did that for us. And God's intention was never our condemnation but salvation. Who wouldn't fall down at the feet of our God and worship! The heart of God is on display before us in this verse. The entirety of the word comes to this verse. This is all of the word before our very eyes. I pray you receive this word afresh at this moment.

The 3:16 Challenge

Reflection

What has been most eye-opening to you in John's gospel? How can this transform your walk with Christ?

_____

_____

_____

_____

_____

_____

_____

_____

_____

_____

_____

_____

Peter's Rebuke

Acts 3:16

Acts 3:16 And his name through faith in his name hath made this man strong, whom ye see and know: yea, the faith which is by him hath given him this perfect soundness in the presence of you all.

Ministry Continues and Grows

The authorship of the book of Acts is attributed to the Apostle Luke. This book opens as Luke writes to Theophilus of those things which occurred in the days in which Christ walked the earth after his resurrection and ultimately ascended to heaven. Acts 1: 5 records these words from Jesus, "For John truly baptized with water; but ye shall be baptized with the Holy Ghost not many days hence." It is this same baptism in the Holy Ghost that believers receive at the moment of their acceptance of Christ and which empowers them with faith to believe those things that we have been endowed with power to do. This is a one time baptism that is not one which can be lost.

It is clear that at this time the apostles still did not fully understand what Jesus' purpose had been here on earth. They were still awaiting the restoration of the governmental authority and kingdom of Israel. Jesus clarifies both his purpose and their calling in the following verses.

Acts 1:6 When they therefore were come together, they asked him, saying, Lord, wilt thou at this time restore again the kingdom to Israel?

They were stuck in the immediacy of their earthly struggles. All they could see was the Roman authority under which they were being suppressed. We are that same way - unable to recognize the bigger picture that Christ is painting for our lives. The daily minutia of our lives can be blinding. The daily grind can be all consuming, so much so that somehow the need for prayer can sometimes allude us. Yet Go is still merciful and bestows upon us another opportunity to walk the path that has been ordained for us.

Acta 1:7 And he said unto them, It is not for you to know the times or the seasons, which the Father hath put in his own power.

Acts 1:8 But ye shall receive power, after that the Holy Ghost is come upon you; and ye shall be witnesses unto me both in Jerusalem, and in all Judea, and in Samaria, and unto the uttermost part of the earth.

They were called to a far greater work than the re-establishment of the kingdom of Israel. The kingdom which they, and we, are called to establish is that which belongs to God. It reaches farther than the borders of any single nation; rather, it expands the entire globe. That is the kingdom we are still called to reach - the entire earthly kingdom must be reached for our Holy God. And after these words were spoken by Jesus he ascended again into the heavens and "...a cloud received him out of their sight" (Acts 1:9). The apostles then set to the task of making right those things which were prophesied about Judas Isacriot, he needed to be replaced after his suicide. Therefore, with Peter in the midst of the about one hundred and twenty which were gathered, they went through the process of selecting the replacement apostle.

Acts 1:21 Wherefore of these men which have companied with us all the time that the Lord Jesus went in and out among us,

Acts 1:22 Beginning from the baptism of John, unto that same day that he was taken up from us, must one be ordained to be a witness with us of his resurrection.

It was critical that these qualifications be met - these candidates had to have an intimate knowledge of Jesus for it was their commission to teach and preach this Jesus to the world. Talk about needing to be the right one for the job! This man must fully be aware of the persecution which would surely come and be willing and able to endure it - this was far more than a notion.

Acts 1:23 And they appointed two, Joseph called Barsabas, who was surnamed Justus, and Matthias.

Acts 1:24 And they prayed, and said, Thou, Lord, which knowest the hearts of all men, shew whether of these two thou hast chosen, Acts 1:25 That he may take part of this ministry and apostleship, from which Judas by transgression fell, that he might go to his own place.

They clearly were approaching this appointment with great seriousness, knowing, to some degree, what fate awaits them anf=d they go forth in prayer to make the best choice of whom God would have.

Acts 1:26 And they gave forth their lots; and the lot fell upon Matthias; and he was numbered with the eleven apostles.

Then their humanity showed up...How, why? Why would you collectively seek God's wisdom in prayer and then cast lots? Why in the world would something this significant be left to chance? Casting lots...seriously? But, alas they succumbed to tradition, this is what they did when making significant decisions. Mathias became the new 12th apostle. The apostles and the disciples were a unified body for the sake of the spread of the gospel and never is that more apparent than in Acts 2.

Acts 2:1 And when the day of Pentecost was fully come, they were all with one accord in one place.

Acts 2:2 And suddenly there came a sound from heaven as a rushing mighty wind, and it filled all the house where they were sitting.

Acts 2:3 And there appeared unto them cloven tongues like as of fire, and it sat upon each of them.

Acts 2:4 And they were all filled with the Holy Ghost, and began to speak with other tongues, as the Spirit gave them utterance.

Now this event is truly remarkable because it was the fulfillment of the promise which Jesus had spoken to them before he ascended into heaven. Also it is remarkable because it speaks to the power of manifestation when believers are on one accord and in one place. My goodness, read again how the Holy Ghost moved in their midst - the power filled the entire house and was visibly manifested above each of them! That would have been amazing enough but the Holy Ghost was not finished with this outpouring yet. Remember, they had been commissioned to preach and teach to the known world. Well there were countless languages in the known world of that day just as there are today. So how would it have been possible to communicate this good news to everyone with such an insurmountable language barrier? God would have to do something that only He could do - destroy all hindrances to his word going forth. And, by His power, that is precisely what happened.

Acts 2:5 And there were dwelling at Jerusalem Jews, devout men, out of every nation under heaven.

Acts 2:6 Now when this was noised abroad, the multitude came together, and were confounded, because that every man heard them speak in his own language.

This is so striking to me as an educator over the past two decades for students that speak multiple languages - it is so difficult to communicate concepts when people do not speak the same language. Imagine the barrier that language would have presented when attempting to communicate the gospel, trying to tell someone about the immaculately conceived Son of God who died and was resurrected on the third day. What if there were no words that translated immaculate, savior, resurrection, or heaven? Quite the barrier right? But the Holy Ghost allowed everyone to hear this good news in their own language. In reading Acts 2:9-11 there are

17 separate locations named throughout what is currently known to be

Asia, Europe, Africa, and the Middle East. Knowing that many languages would be a challenge for us today let alone in ancient times.

Acts 2:12 And they were all amazed, and were in doubt, saying one to another, What meaneth this?

Acts 2:13 Others mocking said, these men are full of new wine The onlookers were more than confused and amazed by the word for in doubt **[1280][diaporeo]** - nonplussed which means to be surprised and confused so much that you do not know how to react. I mean imagine it, here you are in a group of people and another group of folks are all speaking. You're standing next to someone from Turkey, they're standing next to someone from Greece, next to them is someone from

Ethiopia, next to an Iranian and everyone is hearing the speakers in their own native language. Shock and awe is what would be happening. This is what happened that day, and yes, folks from those diverse nations were in that crowd along with Egyptians, Mesopotamians, Libyans, and others.

Acts 2:13 Others mocking said, These men are full of new wine.

These mockers [5512] [**chleuazo**] - to throw out the lip. Can you see this in your mind's eye? These men with their lips poked out thinking the disciples were full of some very strong wine? This had to have been a sight! But Peter stands in defense of his fellow disciples and in defense of scripture which this crowd of devout Jews should have been able to discern.

Acts 2:14 But Peter, standing up with the eleven, lifted his voice, and said unto them, Ye men of Judea, and all ye tha dwelt at Jerusalem, be this known unto you, and hearken to my words:

Acts 2:15 For these are not drunken, as ye suppose, seeing it is bt the third hour of the day.

Acts 2:16 But this is that which was spoken by the prophet Joel.

Acts 2:17 AND IT SHALL COME TO PASS IN THE LAST DAYS, SAITH GOD, I WILL POUR OUT OF M Y SPIRIT UPON ALL FLESH: AND YOUR SONS AND YOUR DAUGHTERS SHALL PROPHESY, AND YOUR YOUNG MEN SHALL SEE VISIONS, AND YOUR OLD MEN SHALL DREAM DREAMS:

Acts 2:18 AND ON MY SERVANTS AND MY HANDMAIDENS I WILL POUR OUT IN THOSE DAYS OF MY SPIRIT; AND THEY SHALL PROPHESY:

Acts 2:19 AND I WILL SHEW WONDERS IN HEAVEN ABOVE, AND SIGNS IN THE EARTH BENEATH; BLOOD, AND FIRE, AND VAPOUR OF SMOKE:

Acts 2:20 THE SUN SHALL BE TURNED INTO DARKNESS, AND THE MOON INTO BLOOD, BEFORE THAT GREAT AND NOTABLE DAY OF THE LORD COME:

Acts 2:21 AND IT SHALL COME TO PASS THAT WHOSOEVER SHALL CALL ON THE NAME OF THE LORD SHALL BE SAVED.

After Peter speaks these words of prophecy to validate the miracle they are all witnessing, he goes on to establish in their hearing exactly who they come in the name of. He calls the name of Jesus of Nazareth and levels the indictment against them for their criminal actions against Christ.

Acts 2:23 Him being delivered by the determinate counsel and foreknowledge of God, ye have taken, and by wicked hands have crucified and slain.

Acts 2:24 Whom God hath raised up, having loosed the pains of death: because it was not possible that he should be holden of it.

Clearly, they know now in whose name Peter and the apostles have come.

Peter refuses to have this miracle maligned as they sought to malign Jesus. He calls their wrong to their faces and goes on to reiterate the prophecies of Christ as spoken through King David whom they acknowledge. David is the acknowledged king through whom the Messiah was to come.

Acts 2:29 Men and brethren, let me freely speak unto you of the patriarch David, that he is both dead and buried, and his sepulchre is with us unto this day.

Acts 2:30 Therefore being a prophet, and knowing that God had sworn with an oath to him, that of the fruit of his loins, according to the flesh, he would raise up Christ to sit on his throne;

Acts 2:31 He seeing this before spake of the resurrection of Christ, and that his soul was not left in hell, neither his flesh did see corruption.

Acts 2:32 This Jesus hath God raised up, whereof we are all witnesses.

Not only has it been clarified of whom they are speaking for, the truth spoke even from what they would have considered antiquity. That truth would never have been considered to be a lie by any devout Jew. Then he says that they, the apostles, are living witnesses to this risen Christ who is a descendant of King David. Yet another undeniable truth. Realizing these facts they did the only thing they could logically do.

Acts 2:37 Now when they heard this, they were pricked to the heart, and said unto Peter and to the rest of the apostles, Men and brethren, what shall we do?

Acts 2:38   Then Peter said unto them, Repent , and be baptized every one of you in the name of Jesus Christ for the remission of your sins, and ye shall receive the gift of the Holy Ghost.

Acts 2:39   For the promise is unto you, and to your children, and to all that are afar off, even as many as the Lord our God shall call.

Acts 2:40   And with many other words did he testify and exhort, saying, Save yourselves from this untoward generation.

Peter did not mince words with them. He preached what was needful and the word, as it always will, found its mark. They saved themselves from the untoward generation. Untoward, [4646] **skolios** - perverse and crooked. That same characteristic is apparent and running rampant in this generation and yet there is time and opportunity for repentance. The body of Christ has got to stand as boldly as Peter did as he proclaimed the truth of Christ; that preached word saved three thousand souls that one day. And they continued that way, on one accord, living in unity of spirit, and preaching the word of God. They were selfless in their giving and everyone had their needs met.

Acts 2:46   And they, continued daily with one accord in the temple, and breaking bread from house to house, did eat their meat with gladness and singleness of heart,

Acts 2:47   Praising God, and having favour with all people. And the Lord added to the church daily such as should be saved.

And the apostles went forward doing that which they had been called to do, preaching repentance from sin and the salvation of the Lord. Chapter 3 opens with an account of the power that Peter and John walked in.

As Peter and John went about their daily ministry in the temple the miraculous happened in the life of one who had been in that same spot for years. Far too often we find ourselves in the same familiar, comfortable spot of complacency. We Just sit waiting for the miraculous to happen upon us when we find that all we had to do in the first place was look up and live.

Acts 3:1   Now Peter and John went up together into the temple at the hour of prayer, being the ninth hour.

Acts 3:2 And a certain man lame from his mother's womb was carried whom they laid daily at the gate of the temple which is called Beautiful, to ask alms of them that entered into the temple;

Ok, I have got to stop and wonder here. Why is it that this man was satisfied with getting close to the house of God but not going in and secondly seeking the help of men and not the salvation of God? How could you be that close to your break-through for years and not reach out and grab for it? I am puzzled by this man's mentality and that of his friends but this is a pervasive mentality - the "That'll do" mentality. I got to church and that'll do. I don't need an actual encounter with the Lord. I'll get this handout from God's people and that'll do. I'm not going to seek God for myself. Why get that close and not reach for God yourself?

It seems that this lame man was so into the mechanical act of asking for alms that he wasn't even making eye contact with those whom he was asking. That speaks volumes for his sense of expectancy; if he truly expected something from anyone he would have been making eye contact with everyone.

Acts 3:3 Who seeing Peter and John about to go into the temple asked an alms.
Acts 3:4 And Peter, fastening his eyes upon him with John, said, Look on us.
Acts 3:5 And he gave heed unto them, expecting to receive something of them.
Acts 3:6 Then Peter said, Silver and gold have I none; but such as I have give I thee: In the name of Jesus Christ of Nazareth rise up and walk. Acts 3:7 And he took him by the right hand, and lifted him up: and immediately his feet and ankle bones received strength.
Acts 3:8 And he leaping stood up, and walked, and entered with them into the temple, walking, and leaping, and praising God

It would be easy to focus on the fact that it was after Peter and John looked at this man that all this happened. That would be an erroneous focus. Likewise it would be wrong to illuminate that the lame man had an expectancy from Peter and John. Guess what, expectancy is often misplaced. So what brought about the miraculous in the life of the lame man, and for Peter and John for that matter? It was the name in which they acted that held the power of manifestation. Peter clarified what he had to offer was nothing material - that's what the lame man expected. The supernatural was about to converge in the natural and the lame man had no idea that his simple act of obedience, looking up at them, was going to bring about a manifestation that he didn't even know he could hope for. Then it happened, the let down turned around. Peter said I have no silver or gold for you -that was the let down. Then came the turn around - but such as I have give I thee: IN THE NAME OF JESUS OF NAZARETH RISE UP AND WALK. My Lord!

Rise up and walk. Something this man had never done before. He doesn't even know how to start - he's been lame from his mother's womb. Rise up and walk - He's never even used his feet and legs like that! Rise up and walk - No one ever told him that was even a possibility for him before. What! But in the name of Jesus - never happens now. In the name of Jesus - what you never knew becomes reality. In the name of Jesus - possibilities manifest in your midst. Peter took the lame man by his right hand, the hand of power, and lifted him up and immediately his feet and ankles received power! This man did what he had never done - he stood, he began to leap, and he walked. He had no idea when he woke up that morning to do what he had always done that God's power would be made manifest miraculously in his life, but it was. When will that day be for you?

Then we see a familiar reaction from the people - amazement. They were amazed because of their perception. It looked like Peter and John had healed this man in their own power. Not so and they are quick to give honor and correction where they are due.

Acts 3:9 And all the people saw him walking and praising God:

Acts 3:10 And they knew that it was he which sat for alms at the Beautiful gate of the temple: and they were filled with wonder and amazement at that which had happened unto him.

Acts 3:11 And as the lame man which was healed hled Peter and John, all the people ran together unto them in the porch that is called Solomon's, greatly wondering.

Acts 3:12 And when Peter saw it, he answered unto the people, Ye men of Israel, why marvel ye at this? Or why look ye so earnestly on us, as though by our own power or holiness we had made this man walk?

People can be so quick to give and take credit yet Peter put the brakes on that in this instance immediately. He would not have it be said that this was done in his power when he knew better. But those who have the gift of healing, or claim so have such, are quick to claim the power is their own. Christ himself declared that power to do greater things would be given to us - things given belong to the one who gives them not the one who receives them. The glory belongs to God. Here Peter sees another opportunity to teach the people a truth that they conveniently seem to have forgotten: this man was healed in the name of Jesus Christ of Nazareth.

Acts 3:13 The God of Abraham, and of Isaac, and of Jacob, the God of our fathers, hath glorified his Son Jesus; whom ye delivered up, and denied him in the presence of Pilate, when he was determined to let him go. Acts 3:14 But ye denied the Holy One and the Just, and desired a murderer to be granted unto you:

Acts 3:15 And killed the Prince of life, whom God hath raised from the dead; whereof we are witnesses.

Acts 3:16 And his name through faith in his name hath made this man strong, whom ye see and know: yea, the faith which is by him hath given him this perfect soundness in the presence of you all.

What a turn these verses present - Peter truly holds nothing back as he brings correction. What is he saying to them? He tells them again that Jesus was the fulfillment of prophecy - the Son of God, the Messiah. He tells them that he was in their midst, on trial for his life though he was innocent and they choose a murderer, Barabas, rather than Christ. Even Pilate saw no just cause to convict Jesus but they sought his life and killed him. He says again that he and the apostles are witnesses to the Risen Savior and it is this same Savior who has healed the lame man in their midst. After this testimony and this proof in their midst there should have been no doubt whatsoever as to how this healing took place. This healing was manifested in the Name of Jesus Christ, our marvelous and miraculous Savior!

Reflection

What has Jesus done in your life that has left you awestruck? You probably won't have space to list it all.

_____

_____

_____

_____

_____

_____

_____

_____

_____

_____

_____

_____

_____

The Penalties of Sin

Romans 3:16

Romans 3:16 Destruction And Misery Are In Their Ways:

Establishing the Faith Among All People

The church at Rome is a very unique burgeoning church in that its birth is thought to have been a direct result of the day of Pentecost. It is believed that believers in Jerusalem who experienced the miraculous events of

Pentecost were so inspired by the preached word that they returned to Roman and planted that church themselves. None of the 12 apostles or the disciples had been sent to Rome on a missionary journey and it was Paul's greatest desire to preach to the believers at Rome. Therefore the introduction to the letter of Romans is an introduction in the truest sense of the word.

The apostle Paul begins by setting forth that he is a legitimate apostle, though he was not one of the original apostles who walked with Jesus he is no less called to be an apostle. He asserts that he is called to preach this same gospel that was prophesied by the prophets of old who shed a light on the Son of God. He is called to preach the same resurrected Christ whom they have confessed their belief in This gospel is for them and for all humanity and is available to them through faith and obedience. He greets them with the love of the Lord. He is so impressed by and grateful for their faith. Our study of Romans will take scriptural study from the Life Application Study Bible: New International Version.

Romans 1:8 First, I thank my God through Jesus Christ for all of you, because your faith is being reported all over the world.

Romans 1:9 God, whom I serve with my whole heart, in preaching the gospel of his Son, is my witness how constantly I remember you Romans 1:10 in my prayers at all times; and I pray that now at last by God's will the way may be opened for me to come to you.

The faith of this church is impressive because they were at the power base of the known world and it was a polytheistic society, Yet here they were being examples of faithfulness to the world! So great was their faithfulness that they had encouraged the man of God and just as much as he felt he could pour into them he felt they could also pour into him. What a testimony of the impact of the day of Pentecost! Paul also wants them to know that it has been his goal for quite some time to get to them but he had been prevented. That has not diminished his desire to come to them - he desperately wants to preach and teach to them.

Romans 1:14 I am obligated both to Greeks and non-Greeks, both to the wise and the foolish.

Romans 1:15 That is why I am so eager to preach the gospel also to you who are at Rome.

Romans 1: 16 I am not ashamed of the gospel, because it is the power of God for the salvation of everyone who believes: first for the Jew, then for the Gentile.

Romans 1:17 For in the gospel a righteousness from God is revealed, a righteousness that is by faith from first to last, just as it is written: "The righteous will live by faith."

Faith is at the heart of Paul's message to the church at Rome and the reality that this is a Gentile body of believers does not diminish God's love for them. The message that he brings establishes that even though salvation was first offered to the Jews it is now available to everyone who believes. Those who are striving to live according to the righteousness of God will live by their faith in him. So what is reserved for those who do not live by faith - the wrath of God.

The wrath of God has been kindled because of man's sinfulness and refusal to acknowledge God for who he is. This is till the case as contemporary man seeks to live in pursuit of our own lusts. For truly the glory of God is all around us though many refuse to acknowledge.

Romans 1:21 For although they knew God, they neither glorified him as God nor gave thanks to him, but their thinking became futile and their foolish hearts were darkened.

Romans 1:22 Although they claimed to be wise, they became fools Romans 1:23 and exchanged the glory of the immortal God for images made to look like mortal man and birds and animals and reptiles.

How can we refuse to live a life that validates our knowledge of God? Why has that been the case throughout human history? Because to acknowledge God diminishes the power and wisdom of man on man. It requires living by a standard that is not developed by man. It requires humility and gratitude and frowns on self gratification and carnality. Living the god-kind of life requires much of us; that much many of us are still unwilling to give up. Though this letter, like all biblical texts, speaks from antiquity, it speaks an undeniable truth.

Romans 1:24 Therefore God gave them over in the sinful desires of their hearts to sexual impurity for the degrading of their bodies with one another. Romans 1:25 They exchanged the truth of God for a lie, and worshipped and served created things rather than the Creator - who is forever praised.
Amen

This is a snapshot from antiquity of modern reality. We have not changed too much over millennia. Sexual perversion is still a thing. Putting the worship of stuff before the worship of God is still a thing. The degradation of our magnificent bodies for whatever reason is still a thing. This behavior is a foul stench in God's nostrils - He hates sin. The closer I get to God the more I hate sin. Paul speaks to the nature of these sexual sins. They include bestiality, homosexuality, and any immoral sexual act. We tend to shine on homosexuality like it is somehow a worse sexual sin but all sexual sins are abominable in God's eyes, regardless of the lies we tell ourselves to justify our behaviors or those we love. We should not condone sin in any form but many of us do. We are better off to tell everyone the reality that God hates sin but not the sinner. There always is a means of escape from sin;

there is always the opportunity for repentance; and there is always our loving God waiting to receive you.

The Apostle Paul holds up a mirror for each of us to examine ourselves in as we read chapter 2. There is little room to argue that he has not made irrefutable points here. We cannot stand in judgment of one another unless we are willing to be judged likewise. Not many of us are willing to be judged as harshly and mercilessly as we judge others, hold on to that reality.

Romans 2:1 You, therefore, have no excuse, you who pass judgment on someone else, for whatever point you judge the other, you are condemning yourself, because you who pass judgment do the same things.

Now let's just sit with this verse for a moment as it continues to sting. This is us, all judging others without that all important self reflection and examination. How easy it is to point those fingers at others, so critical, harsh, mean, and hypocritical. Yep...Paul found us where we live and kicked down the door. And he is right, when God meets out judgment we get what we deserve though he does tend to show us the mercy we refuse others. I have been that woman - looking at other women with such contempt. Why? I saw too much of myself in them. Didn't like it one bit. I could see how wrong they were...and told them to their faces while I was that same chic and hating me for it. My LORD. God showed me that chic one day and I was truly ashamed and I had no choice but to repent of my mess. But the damage had already been done. Thank God for affording me an opportunity to live past my whorishness and willfulness. I thank him that he gave me an opportunity to stop living the lies I was telling myself and allowing others to believe. He taught me that what I was aspiring to was so little - sin makes us so very small. He had so much more for me. He has more for you. When we drop the judgmental facade, and we see ourselves, then God can use us, even the past we would rather hide away, to minister to someone else who is where we have been. Remember the words of Romans 2:6, "God "will give to each person according to what he has done."

I remember many years ago having a conversation with someone on the topic of forgiveness. More to the point, when it was inappropriate for a sinner to ask for forgiveness for the sins of their lives. This person asserted that it was unfair for the worst sinners to live terribly and ask for and receive forgiveness on their deathbed. My contention was who are we to think that God should withhold forgiveness, whenever it is sought? I pointed out that the thief who hung next to Jesus on Calvary asked Jesus to remember him and was told that he would be with him that day in glory. You can't get any closer to your eternity than that and get snatched away from hell's fires. He was sincere and was forgiven. Some people get it before others but they still come to the realization that they need repentance and do it. They receive the blessing of forgiveness and I bless God for all who seek and receive it. I have been on the receiving end and want that for everyone who needs it. That is the heart of the issue for me. I think the other individual left feeling displeased with my response but I know God was pleased. We are called to repentance...period.

Romans 2:7 To those who by persistence in doing good seek glory, honor and immortality, he will give eternal life.

Romans 2:8 But to those who are self-seeking and who reject the truth and follow evil, there will be wrath and anger.

Romans 2:9 There will be trouble and distress for every human being who does evil: first for the Jew, then for the Gentile;

Romans 2:10 but glory, honor and peace for everyone who does good: first for the Jew, then for the Gentile.

Romans 2:11 For God does not show favoritism.

The issue of favoritism was a huge issue but not nearly as huge as the rift created by those who esteemed the law above all else. The keeping of the law was critical in the walk of the devout Jew, as it should have been, But it should not have become the "gotcha" that it had become for those who gave lip service to it but in truth did not abide by it. The most pressing issue between Jews and Gentiles was the issue of circumcision - this cutting of the flesh which was held as a sign of devout Judaism. This physical act, the cutting of the foreskin, was being required by some before they could even fully be accepted into the body of Christ. This was a perversion of what Christ himself had taught and expected. This, coupled with the strict keeping of the law, was becoming a stumbling block for many who wanted nothing more than to be a part of the Church. But the greatest hindrance was that they could clearly see the hypocrisy of some of the Jews who professed this devotion while being lawbreakers. Paul addresses this issue quite plainly.

Romans 2:28 A man is not a Jew if he is only one outwardly, nor is circumcision merely outward and physical.

Romans 2:29 No, a man is a Jew if he is one inwardly; and circumcision is circumcision of the heart, by the Spirit, not by written code. Such a man's praise is not from men, but from God.

The circumcision that we all must seek, women included, is a heart issue. There are things that each of us must purge and excise from our hearts; things that have prevented us from walking this journey and shining our lights in this world. Only you know what needs to be circumcised from your heart, you and God that is, so go on and cut those things away. Is there some additional value that this circumcision can add to our lives or conversion to Judaism? These are the questions that lead us into the third chapter of Romans.

Romans 3:1 What advantage, then, is there in being a Jew, or what value is there in circumcision?

Romans 3:2 Much in every way! First of all, they have been entrusted with the very words of God.

It is so important to understand who Paul is - he is a Jew among Jews. His pedigree is impeccable and he was known for his zeal. He is a proud Jew and he knows his heritage and the calling that was entrusted to the Jewish people - they are God's chosen people. They were to bring the news of God to all humanity. And what about those who did not hold up their end of that bargain, did that end it for everyone else? Absolutely not. What their failure did was give everyone else the opportunity to do what they should have done. Yet, even with their failing God did not throw them away - He did exactly what he said he would do. God is not a covenant breaker!

Romans 3:3 What if some did not have faith? Will their lack of faith nullify God's faithfulness?

Romans 3:4 Not at all! Let God be true, and every man a liar. As it is written: "So that you may be proved right when you speak and prevail when you judge."

Paul then goes into the argument that the unrighteousness of man is not overlooked by our righteous God. Many would argue today that our loving God will simply forgive our continued sin. God does forgive but there are always repercussions for sin. God does not turn a blind eye to our sin because of His love for us - he gives us the opportunity to repent. God is not glorified by man's sin. Paul had to correct a misunderstanding of what was being reported as his teaching on this issue. Read these scriptures closely:

Romans 3:5 But if our unrighteousness brings out God's righteousness more clearly, what shall we say? That God is unjust in bringing his wrath on us? (I am using a human argument.)

Romans 3:6 Certainly not! If that were so, how could God judge the world?

Romans 3:7 Someone might argue, "If my falsehood enhances God's truthfulness and so increases his glory, why am I still condemned as a sinner?"

Romans 3:8 Why not say-as we are being slanderously reported as saying and as some claim that we say- "Let us do evil that good may result"? Their condemnation is deserved.

This false teaching could have destroyed this newborn church had it not been corrected in this letter. As ridiculous as it sounds, for those who had malintentions for the church, the confusion could have been just enough to dissuade some folks from seeking for themselves. But this lie struck right at the heart of the call and need for repentance. It suggests that it was fine to keep living a life of sin and God would be alright with that. Your life would give evidence of his forgiving nature and his acceptance of your sin - What a LIE! Although it would seem that this mindset has infiltrated the body of Christ again as the hypocritical lifestyle is on full display in many churches.

Perpetuating this kind of lie with one's lifestyle will not go unnoticed by God. Paul further asserts that everyone, both Jew and Gentile, is under sin. We are still under sin today. Again we are shown a snapshot that is as relevant today as it was in antiquity:

Romans 3:11 "... there is no one who **understands**, no one who **seeks** God.

What is Paul saying here? There is no one who **understands/suniemi [4920] (to put together mentally),** no one who **seeks/ekzeteo [1567] (to seek out, investigate, crave, demand carefully and diligently).** I feel this verse because opportunities to study God's word are the most poorly attended meetings in the body of Christ. Paul certainly spoke a truth that is sadly still true today. Lord, that we would seek you more. These are hard truths that bring us to our key scripture as he points out that the law does not bring about righteousness; rather, it brings about the awareness of sin. It is this awareness of sin, our very sin nature, that should cause us to run into the arms of our God. Unfortunately, our bad situations are only worsened by sin:

Romans 3:12 All have turned away, they have together become worthless; there is no one who does good, not even one."

Romans 3:13 "Their throats are open graves; their tongues practice deceit." "The poison of vipers is on their lips."

Romans 3:14 "Their mouths are full of cursing and bitterness."

Romans 3:15 "Their feet are swift to shed blood; **Romans 3:16 ruin and misery mark their ways,**

Romans 3:17 and the way of peace they do not know.

It breaks my heart to read these words, written thousands of years ago, and to realize that it is as if Paul walked our streets today. My spirit longs for those who are being denigrated by their sin to just understand their need for repentance and for them to actually repent. Lord, that they would repent. Lord that we all repent of our sin daily if need be. God be merciful to us as we seek you more diligently. Help us to know your ways, that we not suffer under the law but that we flourish by your grace. Lord that we truly come to know your peace. Amen.

The 3:16 Challenge

Write a prayer of REFLECTION.

_____

_____

_____

_____

_____

_____

_____

_____

_____

_____

_____

_____

_____

Self Knowledge

I Corinthians 3:16

I Corinthians 3:16 Know ye not that ye are the temple of God, and that the Spirit of God dwelleth in you?

The Message, Not the Messenger

The Apostle Paul had such an extremely challenging role in the growing Church, he was essentially the traveling overseer. He got word of the successes, the troubles, the conflicts, the growth, the confusion - you name it and Paul responded. The church at Corinth was no different. It was located on the coastline of the Aegean Sea, which means it was an important port city. Having been raised in a port city, New Orleans, Louisiana, I understand what that means. There is a flood of people from everywhere and they bring the influence of their traditions, cultures, religions, all that they are. Corinth is likely to have had a very similar reality. Paul, after his words of greetings, is quick to extol them for their faithfulness and to offer edification through the Lord Jesus Christ. He wastes no time addressing one of the main issues that led him to write to them - the reported divisions in the church.

I Corinthians 1:10 I appeal to you, brothers, in the name of our Lord Jesus Christ, that all of you agree with one another so that there may be no divisions among you and that you may be perfectly united in mind and judgment.

This is a huge appeal for any people in any regard - agreement for the sake of unity for the sake of thoughts, will, and purpose. Without this agreement as a starting point nothing else will flourish, the church would die on the proverbial vine. And what is at the heart of the division that is plaguing the Corinthian church? Leadership loyalties. Some were proclaiming their loyalties to one leader and others to another leader. Paul is clearly perturbed because the eyes of them all should have been on Christ as they received the preached and ministered word from their leaders as they themselves followed Christ. They needed a reality check and this letter delivers this one:

I Corinthians 1:13 Is Christ divided? Was Paul crucified for you? Were you baptized into the name of Paul?

I Corinthians 1:17 For Christ did not send me to baptize, but to preach the gospel - not with words of human wisdom, lest the cross of Christ be emptied of its power.

Perspective and purpose unashamedly delivered. Paul's perspective is that Christ is unified and singular of purpose. Paul's purpose is to preach the gospel. That in and of itself is so preeminent there shouldn't be time for anything petty. Preaching and teaching Christ should be consuming their energies and their efforts but somehow their focus had been lost. We too, sometimes tend to get caught up in the sauce of messenger over message.

But it is the message that should be the draw. The good news of Jesus Christ should be the headliner. The marquee should boast of his appearance. The accolades should ring out for all Jesus has done. The messengers are necessary but the focus should be the word! It is so easy to be drawn to a person, as if they are empowered to give life but life is in the word.

Countless people have been led astray when what they needed most was the word of life. They needed to be taught what they did not yet understand. They needed to be fed because their souls were starving for nourishment. They needed true leadership of the Savior not hero worship of a minister. Unfortunately when some don't get what they actually need when they are at those critical moments, they fall away forever. Lord, that we never be the cause of anyone being lost.

I Corinthians 1:18 For the message of the cross is foolishness to those who are perishing, but to us who are being saved it is the power of God. **I Corinthians 1:25** For the foolishness of God is wiser than man's wisdom, and the weakness of God is stronger than man's strength.

Paul then calls on them to remember from whence they had come. We do well to do likewise. Just consider who you were before you knew Christ - how lost, sad, weak, fraudulent and Christ changed all that. Every good thing that we are and ever will become is due to Christ and it is in him that we should boast, not in or of ourselves. God gets the glory!

Chapter 2 provides the text for one of my favorite sermons, "All I know is Jesus". I reflect on Paul's words to the church, how he tells them in all sincerity how he presented Christ to them. He didn't do it for the accolades. He didn't do it so that men would follow him. He didn't do it to sound deep and profound. He wasn't being philosophical. None of that. It was clear for him and he needs it to be clear for them.

I Corinthians 2:1 When I came to you, brothers, I did not come with eloquence or superior wisdom as I proclaimed to you the testimony about God.

I Corinthians 2:2 For I resolved to know nothing while I was with you except Jesus Christ and him crucified.

I Corinthians 2:3 I came to you in weakness and fear, and with much trembling.

I Corinthians 2:4 My message and my preaching were not ith wise or persuasive words, but with a demonstration of the Spirit's power,

I Corinthians 2:5 so that your faith might not rest on men's wisdom, but on God's power.

When you know your purpose nothing can dissuade you from it. When it's about Jesus - it's about Jesus. I don't want to hear that I did well - The Spirit did well in me. When Paul delivered the word it wasn't to impress them with himself but rather to impress upon them the life-changing reality that the Savior was being offered to them. It wasn't for him to appear wise in their eyes but for them to see the wisdom of accepting Jesus and repenting of their sin. The goal was not for them to put their faith and trust in Paul. To the contrary, it was for them to be open to putting their faith and trust in our Holy God. It's more than the simplistic idol worship that their culture was prone to indulging in, just as ours is prone to as well.

I Corinthians 2:9 However, as it is written: "No eye has seen, no ear has heard, no mind has conceived what God has prepared for those who love him"

I Corinthians 2:10 but God has revealed it to us by his Spirit.

We are to seek the guidance and instruction of the Spirit as he leads us in all wisdom and discernment. It is the Spirit that illuminates the truth and mysteries of God for us. But the man or woman who does not have the Spirit of God will not understand the things of God because they simply cannot. It's foolishness to them and will be until they have the Spirit indwelling them. Until that is the reality we are worldly.

I Corinthians 3:1 Brothers, I could not address you as spiritual but as worldly - mere infants in Christ.

I Corinthians 3:2 I gave milk, not solid food, for you were not ready for it.

I have heard these scriptures preached and taught many times as though they were intended to demean the church at Corinth. There is more here than that because any good leader has to discern when his or her people are prepared to receive. The proper nourishment is relative to the person being fed. That is why there are so many varieties of foods to choose from - everyone can't handle everything. Babies are not born prepared to ingest burgers nor are teenagers solely sustained on milk. The analogy resonates with me as a mom who understands keenly about the difficulty of feeding her babies.

Feeding the three daughters who have been born to me was a struggle. From breastfeeding to formula feeding it was just a struggle knowing what would nourish them. For my first born, Namandje, I wanted so badly to breastfeed her but my milk wouldn't come. Then I bottle fed her and she vomited more than she got for the first weeks of her life. Then, at 3 weeks, the pediatrician said, "Give her food." I was stunned - how could she be ready for that? Wasn't it too soon? Was that the best thing for her? It was rough, the vomiting continued, projectile vomiting, until her stomach muscles were strong enough to hold the food down, about three weeks later. But she soon began to flourish to my very pleasant surprise.

My younger two daughters, Grace and Rhema, I was able to breastfeed but then I couldn't produce enough milk to keep up with them and had to supplement. Again I tried formula and both of them were allergic to every single formula and I had to learn how to make their food. I finally settled on whole milk and fresh fruit - more fruit than milk- and that worked for them until they got to solid food. Nourishment for infants can be very, very tricky. Even though that is the case, they still need what they need and it changes when they can, watch this, handle more. That is what I feel Paul is getting to - he gave them, the church at Corinth, what they could handle.

Is that to suggest that they should never have been ready for the strong meat? Absolutely not. Neither is that a suggestion that those among us in our congregations who are still sucking on milk are getting the nourishment that they need. As I learned from my babies, the time came when they could handle more and we gave them the more. Their bodies had been fortified by the milk and supplements as long as they could, for any longer would have stunted their growth. I certainly did not want to stunt them, they were going to be small anyway because we, their parents, are small. They needed to flourish. Just as the body of Christ is stunted when not presented with the proper diet of word. But sometimes radical approaches have to be taken to promote growth.

One of our daughters was the tiniest of them all and I was concerned that she might have been a dwarf. I shared my concerns with the pediatrician and she suggested something radical. Dr. Gandhi, I'll never forget her, suggested that I try what the women of her Hindu culture had suggested to help small infants grow. She advised me to put her in the window and let the sun shine on her. I know what you're thinking, and you may even be chuckling, I did, thinking she was joking but she didn't crack a smile. She said it again, looking me in my eyes and playing with Grace's little feet "Put her in the window and let the sun shine on her for as long as she will tolerate it every day." "Ok. I trust you." I went home and put the baby in the window for weeks and when we brought her back she had grown more than in any previous visit. Yes. It worked. Radical and effective. What does any of this have to do with this letter to the Corinthians? They needed a radical approach to meet their unique needs.

They had been getting some worldliness in what should have been an exclusively spiritual diet. They were so distracted by the messengers that they were completely "word" malnourished. So, like Jesus, Paul uses a parable here that is readily understood. Everyone would have understood what it takes for crops to grow successfully and he presents this imagery to them. It is a task that requires multiple workers to be successful. However even with the best efforts of the workers there are those unseen forces in the earth that also work to bring about growth. When it comes to the work of the ministry God has a need for the hands, feet, and mouths of humanity and the internal work is done by the Holy Spirit of God. That is how the increase is made manifest in the lives of the church.

I Corinthians 3:5 What, after all, is Apollos? And what is Paul? Only servants, through whom you came to believe - as the Lord has assigned to each his task.

I Corinthians 3:6 I planted the seed, Apollos watered it, but God made it grow.

I Corinthians 3:7 So neither he who plants nor he who waters is anything, but only God, who makes things grow.

There is so much that the Corinthian church had missed by the distractions of focus on leadership and other causes of division among them. They should have been in the building phase, where the church was growing exponentially but that was not yet possible because their foundational understanding was still quite unstable. Therefore Paul inserts another analogy - the laying of a solid foundation for a building. He offers a warning about building another foundation on one which has been previously laid.

I Corinthians 3:11 For no one can lay any foundation other than the one already laid, which is Jesus Christ.

I Corinthians 3:12 If any man builds on this foundation using gold, silver, costly stones, wood, hay, or straw,

I Corinthians 3:13 his work will be shown for what it is, because the Day will bring it to light. It will be revealed with fire, and the fire will test the quality of each man's work.

I Corinthians 3:14 If what he has built survives, he will receive his reward. **I Corinthians 3:15** If it is burned up, he will suffer loss; he himself will be saved, but only as one escaping through the flames.

I Corinthians 3:16 Don't you know that you yourselves are God's temple and that God's Spirit lives in you?

I Corinthians 3:17 If anyone destroys God's temple, God will destroy him; for God's temple is sacred, and you are that temple.

There is great work to be done in us just as there was great work to be done in them. This message resonates today as we come to know how much God loves us and desires to be in relationship with us. How can I make that claim? Easily, everything that Paul points to in these opening chapters of this letter are relational issues. If the church did not address those relational issues within themselves they would never get to the relationship that God had in store for them. Each of these first three chapters highlights a different aspect of this relationship between the church at Corinth and God right up to our pivotal verse.

1. **Getting to Know You** - This church could not get to know Jesus because they were being blocked by those who wanted to take the glory from Jesus.

2. **Too into Them** - They struggled hearing the word clearly because they were simply too into the messengers and not enough into the message.

3. **Time to Grow Up and Glow Up**- They did not recognize that they were missing key milestones in their relationship with God. It was clearly time to grow up in the relationship but they were malnourished, unsure of how growth should happen, and unskilled at building.

Reflection

How has this study shown you areas of growth for your relationship both in your local assembly and with God?

_____

_____

_____

_____

_____

_____

_____

_____

_____

_____

_____

_____

Taking Away the Vail

II Corinthians 3:16

II Corinthians 3:16 Nevertheless when it shall turn to the Lord, the vail shall be taken away.

Sometimes You Just Need to Explain

The Corinthian church was still in an unsettled state. This carries over from the first letter which Paul had written to them - there were some hard feelings and misunderstandings. Over great distances this is quite understandable. Therefore Paul offers a greeting that is typical for him and he wastes little time putting forth his position - God is compassionate and comforting to his children. Clearly he felt the need to initiate this conversation from that position of both humility and strength. His position is both of these because his foundation is God, the Father of Jesus Christ whom he had preached into their hearing. They have benefitted together from God's comfort and should be willing to extend this to others as they have need of it.

II Corinthians 1:3 Praise be to the God and Father of our Lord Jesus Christ, the Father of compassion and the God of all comfort, II Corinthians 1:4 who comforts us in all our troubles, so that we can comfort those in any trouble with the comfort we ourselves have received from God.

It's a friendly reminder that we all need compassion from time to time on our Christian journey. If God almighty can bestow this upon us surely we can do the same in times of trouble for each other. We do well to listen to the teaching and apply it liberally to our own lives. Those who are called into leadership suffer greatly for God's people, often in silence, but the people should recall their own humanity extends to their leaders. Life happens and circumstances intrude upon ministry - we who serve are in need of the same compassion that we extend both in prayer and deed. He expresses the idea that when one suffers we all suffer just as when one rejoices we all rejoice. Paul has endured some horrendous trials for the cause of Christ on his ministerial journeys in Asia; he shares this with them.

II Corinthians 1:8 We do not want you to be uninformed, brothers, about the hardships we suffered in the province of Asia. We were under great pressure, far beyond our ability to endure, so that we despaired even of life. II Corinthians 1:9 Indeed, in our hearts we felt the sentence of death. But this happened that we might not rely on ourselves but on God, who raises the dead.

II Corinthians 1:10 He has delivered us from such a deadly peril, and he will deliver us. On him we have set our hope that he will continue to deliver us, II Corinthians 1:11 as you help us by your prayers. Then many will give thanks on our behalf for the gracious favor granted us in answer to the prayers of many.

We may never know all that each of us endures privately, and there honestly is no need to know. There is, however, the sincere need for constant prayer because our earnest prayers go places we may never reach. Our prayers bring rescue, comfort, release from all manner of pain, we may never know what our prayers do in the spirit realm but we do know we ought to always pray for one another. Paul offers a perfect illustration of that fact. Their prayers got him through situations when he knew he didn't have the strength to endure on his own. Those prayers reached the very throne of God and he moved on Paul's behalf. It works that same way when we seek God in prayer for one another.

The adversary uses people to mount all kinds of attacks against God's people and it seems Paul"s reputation, calling, and ministry were being relentlessly attacked. Maybe his past was coming back to haunt him; folks can sometimes begrudge you the grace God grants to bring about life change. Some folks make it their life mission to resurrect the you who was the worst representation of godliness. You may be able to relate to Paul's struggle with this church - I certainly can. These attacks are designed to hurt and they do. They are designed to shame and they do. They are orchestrated to cast doubt and they do. But thanks be unto God these weapons that are formed against us shall not prosper. They did not when hurled at Paul and they will not when they come against you or me. Amen His integrity was under attack - the sincerity of his word. If his word could be questioned then so could his ministry. The defense that he mounts is deftly executed and well warranted. This church needed to be firm in their trust in Paul and Timothy, in that they had planned to come in support of them. They didn't do so lightly; they didn't brush them off. Clearly the issues that had been addressed in the first letter and during the first visit had not been resolved. He thought it wisest not to return at that time. Sometimes we have to know when to allow the passage of time.

II Corinthians 1:23 I call God as my witness that it was in order to spare you that I did not return to Corinth.

He did what he felt was best and he stood on that.

This explanation continues into the second chapter and is further elucidated for them. He has no intention of being a source of grief because they had already experienced some grief as a church body and this grievance has been forgiven. This episode tested them tremendously. Congregations everywhere will face similar challenges and will need to exhibit genuine forgiveness in order to grow in the grace of God. What a deep lesson that is a forever requirement of God's people.

II Corinthians 2:9 The reason I wrote to you was to see if you would stand the test and be obedient in everything.
II Corinthians 2:10 If you forgive anyone, I also forgive him. And what I have forgiven-if there was anything to forgive- I have forgiven in the sight of
Christ for your sake,
II Corinthians 2:11 in order that Satan might not outwit us. For we are not unaware of his schemes.

What wisdom! When troubles arise be sure that you focus on the true source of the trouble. Though human agents may be used to carry out the plan - be very sure that when God's people are attacked, the adversary is unseen - Satan. He needs those who are willing to be used by him to bring his plots to fruition. It's easy to focus our anger on the person you see but they are being used masterfully by our true adversary - Satan. From the issue of forgiveness the chapter moves to a close with the troubling allegation of ministry for profit.

Chapter 3 opens with a troubling question that alludes to the reemergence of some shady behaviors. Some were going out to preach with "commendations" from the church. These people were using letters of introduction in the name of the church to go out and preach for pay. Those who would abuse the gospel have been around from the very earliest planting of the church. They were incompetent in the ministry and sought only to serve themselves; this is prevalent in churches today, sadly.

II Corinthians 3:1 Are we beginning to commend ourselves again? Or do we need, like some people, letters of recommendation to you or from you? II Corinthians 3:2 You yourselves are our letter, written on our hearts, known and read by everybody.

II Corinthians 3:3 You show that you are a letter from Christ, the result of our ministry, written not with ink but with the Spirit of the living God, not on tablets of stone but on the tablets of human hearts.

The greatest endorsement of any ministry will always be the people and their works. Once it is shed abroad, outside the four walls, impacting the community and by extension the world, that is all that is necessary. True God ordained ministry does not need an introduction - it introduces itself to the world boldly and with power. The Spirit will illuminate it for all to see. The newness that comes by God's free gift of grace will open to everyone with nothing being hidden. True ministers of God will withhold nothing from God's people because the veil has been torn asunder.

Somehow the old teachings were creeping back into the church at Corinth and this idea that all people did not have access was emerging again. They did not fully understand that they were at liberty to have a true relationship with God the Father, his Son Jesus Christ, and the Holy Spirit. They expected the veil to still be intact though it no longer existed.

II Corinthians 3:12 Therefore, since we have such a hope, we are very bold.

II Corinthians 3:13 We are not like Moses, who would put a veil over his face to keep the Iraelites from gazing at it while the radiance was fading away.

II Corinthians 3:14 But their minds were made dull, for to this day the same veil remains when the old covenant is read. It has not been removed, because only in Christ is it taken away.

II Corinthians 3:15 Even to this day when Moses is read a veil covers their hearts.

II Corinthians 3:16 But whenever anyone turns to the Lord, the veil is taken away.

II Corinthians 3:17 Now the Lord is the Spirit, and where the Spirit of the Lord is, there is freedom.

Modern believers exist with the same idea to some degree. The veil no longer exists. You have access to Jesus Christ. Somehow the notion persists that only some people have access to the Savior - not true. The idea is swimming around in the heads of many that they are not equipped to go to Jesus in prayer for themselves, that he won't hear them. That they don't have access to the Holy of Holies. That the veil prevents their falling on their knees before the father. None, I repeat, none of that is true. Once you come to accept the Lord Jesus Christ you are baptized in the Holy Spirit and you have the liberty that sets all the captives free! The Veil Is Gone! Enter in and worship him!

Reflection

What has hindered your access to Jesus? Whatever it may have been, just know that when you gave your life to Christ, at that very moment, you had the freedom to seek him for yourself. Nothing prevents you from reaching Christ. There is absolutely no barrier to you entering into this relationship and fellowship with Jesus.

_____

_____

_____

_____

_____

_____

_____

_____

_____

_____

_____

_____

The Promise to the Seed
Galatians3:16

Galatians 3:16 Now to Abraham and his seed were the promises made. He saith not, And to seeds, as of many; but as of one, AND TO THY SEED, which is Christ.

The Heart of the Issue

I'm not an individual who likes to beat around the bush, that's a waste of time. And my students will tell you that they have heard my personal mantra frequently - "Time is the one commodity in life we can't get back so don't waste mine." I mean that whole heartedly. Time is precious and we are not cognizant of how much God has granted to us - use it wisely. That's why I adore the way Paul writes his letters, efficiently. He identifies himself, greets the church, then cuts to the chase. It's a formula and it works.

Galatians 1:6 I am astonished that you are so quickly deserting the one who called you by the grace of Christ and are turning to a different gospel - Galatians 1:7 which is really no gospel at all. Evidently some people are throwing you into confusion and are trying to pervert the gospel of Christ.

It is amazing and very disconcerting that anyone who had received the gospel could be persuaded by something different. Or is it? I can think of cults that emerged during my lifetime that had leaders who professed to be following the gospel. People believed in their message. People left everything and followed them. People were deceived, some lost their possessions, some lost their lives. But how? Why didn't they know better in an age where the word was literally at your fingertips? They depended on others to tell them rather than learning, seeking, and studying for themselves. They had no excuse not to know. This is not new in the 21st century but in the 1st century it was.

The 1st century church was in its infancy. It was in direct competition, if you will, with Judaism and they did not want to lose any of their faithful. And yet they were; many were converting from Judaism to Christianity. Release from the impossible burden of the Law must have been intoxicating! Who wouldn't want to revel in the freedom afforded believers in Jesus Christ? Even some who wanted freedom found it cumbersome to relinquish who they were because of the Law. The Law was clean cut. You could be established because you adhered to the letter of the Law. It was easier to claim righteousness under the Law - it could be seen, you could be seen. Many Jewish believers, especially the religious leaders, were enamored with the notion of being seen, being more holy than others, appearing closer to God than others because they could boldly proclaim that they obeyed the Law which God had given to Moses. They could most proudly signify their holiness because they were circumcised and that, under Mosaic Law, along with the keeping of all the other hundreds of laws, kept you in right standing with God. But this gospel effectively did away with that and some tried to undermine it by mixing the old way of the Law with the new way of Christ. Paul's position is abundantly clear on the issue:

Galatians 1:9 As we have already said, so now I say again: If anybody is preaching to you a gospel other than what you accepted, let him be eternally condemned!

Further evidence of his sincerity of conversion to this calling is Paul's revelation, though it was widely known, of how zealously he had persecuted the church before his own conversion. His entire mission was to utterly destroy the church in his zeal for Judaism. He was greatly feared because of his adherence to the Law and customs of his beliefs. Inexplicably, God chose him to be an apostle for the spread of this same gospel. He went from the greatest prosecutor of the church to its greatest advocate and defender. Only God can bring about that kind of magnificent change in someone's life. He immediately began to do the work of ministry among the Gentiles.

Galatians 1:15 But when God, who set me apart from birth and called me by his grace, was pleased

Galatians 1:16 to reveal his Son in me so that I might preach him among the Gentiles, I did not consult any man,

Galatians 1:17 nor did I go to Jerusalem to see those who were apostles before I was, but I went immediately into Arabia and later returned to Damascus.

These verses are so important to understand because both the validity of his calling and his ministry had been called into question. But like the other apostles Paul had also been hand picked - the Damascus Road experience is all the validation he will ever need. God plucked him off that donkey while he was on his way to persecute the church vigorously and his whole life got turned around. He did not need anyone else's stamp of approval to do what God had appointed for his hands to do. God uses whomever he chooses to accomplish his work on this earth.

Chapter 2 has Paul, Barnabas, and Titus going to Jerusalem after fourteen years of ministry to preach the gospel which he had been preaching to the Gentiles. It is there that he is confronted with this mixed gospel that was requiring Gentiles to be circumcised before accepting Jesus Christ. This was a clear perversion of the pure gospel; there was no requirement of circumcision before accepting Christ. Perhaps this started as an honest mistake since the original apostles had been practicing Judaism before they began to follow Christ. That was not a requirement that Jesus had imposed on them - it simply was their reality. But this was then being forcibly imposed on Gentile converts to Christianity by Judaizers - Jews who converted to Christianity. It was an unnecessary "flaming hoop" that they were being made to jump through. So Paul and Titus went directly to the leadership.

Galatians 2:1 Then after fourteen years I again went up to Jerusalem with Barnabas, taking Titus along also.

Galatians 2:2 I went up in accord with a revelation, and presented to them the gospel that I preach to the Gentiles-but privately to those of repute-so that I might not be running, or have run, in vain.

Galatians 2:3 Moreover, not even Titus, who was with me, although he was a Greek, was compelled to be circumcised,

Galatians 2:4 but because of the false brothers secretly brought in, who slipped in to spy on our freedom that we have in Christ Jesus, that they might enslave us-

Galatians 2:5 to them we did not submit even for a moment, so that the truth of the gospel might remain intact for you

His steadfastness made it obvious to James, Cephas, and John that Paul's ministry to the Gentiles was equally as valid as Peter's was to the Jews. That same day they gave Paul and Barnabas the right hand of fellowship to minister to the Gentiles, asking only that they remember the poor. However it was clear that the issue of the circumcision versus the uncircumcision had not been resolved because Paul confronted Peter in Antioch.

On this occasion the issue was Peter's sincerity when in mixed company, meaning Jewish Christians and Gentile converts. Peter would not eat with the Gentile converts when the Jewish Christians were around - he seemed clearly uncomfortable to eat the Gentile converts in their presence. Well Paul called him out on that publically. The hypocrisy of Peter and the others even caused Barnabas to backslide but Paul was right to address them.

Galatians 2:15 We who are Jews by birth and Gentile sinners

Galatians 2:16 know that a man is not justified by observing the law, but by faith in Jesus Christ.

So it comes down to the all important idea of righteousness: how can one be made righteous? According to the Law you had to obey the Law in its entirety. That is it - righteousness by obedience. How is that opposed to grace? Grace is not legalistic. Grace does not morph by the manipulations of man. Grace is a free gift that comes from God when you confess your belief in Jesus Christ. It knows no limits. It is not exclusive. You can not out grace someone else. Rather than being a thing that binds, the gift of God is liberating. Justification is included in that package because you need not make any sacrifice for your sin - Jesus already paid the cost. There is not one thing that we could ever do to be made righteous in God's eyes. Jesus's death, burial, and resurrection did that. Being in Christ causes justification to be made manifest in you. Jesus changed the whole religious structure. The Holy Spirit who indwells us has allowed access to the secret things. God has extended himself, through Jesus Christ, to all who would receive him. This is the beauty of the gospel that was being preached to the Gentiles - LIBERTY IN CHRIST!

Why does chapter 3 open with such a harsh statement followed by an equally harsh question?

Galatians 3:1 You foolish Galatians! Who has **bewitched** you? Before your very eyes Jesus Christ was clearly portrayed as crucified.

Let's examine this word **bewitch**. Strong's Exhaustive Concordance defines it as follows - baskaino [940] to slander, to bewitch; give the evil eye to captivate; appealing to someone's vanity and selfishness. Each of these explanations is an excellent example of the motivation for what was happening in this young church in Galatia, however the last seems to hit the nail on the head. They, those who were unwilling to welcome new believers in with sincerity, were simply selfish. It could be that they felt it unfair for Gentiles to have access to God. It could be that they felt they should have to endure all the ritualistic practices that they had. It could be that they wanted the freedom of Christ for themselves only. It could be that they didn't want them at all. Whatever the case was it was selfish to hinder any believer from coming to Christ and yet this had persisted. Sadly, this selfish, egotistical, divisive mindset exists in various forms today in the contemporary church as many find reasons to turn those in dire need of the Savior away.

Galatians 3:2 I would like to learn just one thing from you: Did you receive the Spirit by observing the law, or by believing what you heard?
Galatians 3:3 Are you so foolish? After beginning with the Spirit, are you now trying to attain your goal by human effort?

Wow! Just wow. This church is so thoroughly confused that they are falling back to old, ineffective, habitual, legalistic behavior. Why is this happening? Because these ideas were so radically simple to execute - believe and receive - that there just had to be more to it. There had to be more for them to do...right? There has to be more for us to do...right? It cannot be that straightforward, that simple, that genuine...can it? Why would God make it that easy? Why not?

Galatians 3:6 Consider Abraham: He believed God, and it was credited to him as righteousness.

Galatians 3:7 Understand, then, that those who believe are children of Abraham.

Galatians 3:8 The Scripture foresaw that God would justify the Gentiles by faith, and announced the gospel in advance to Abraham: "All nations will be blessed through you."

Galatians 3:9 So those who have faith are blessed along with Abraham, the man of faith.

Galatians 3:10 All who rely on observing the law are under a curse, for it is written: "Cursed is everyone who does not continue to do everything written in the Book of the Law."

Galatians 3:11 Clearly no one is justified before God by the law, because,

"The righteous will live by faith."

Now Paul brings his argument to the heart of Judaism ancestry, pride, and belief. This is a turning point in defense of the gospel he has preached before the Gentiles. He points to the fact that Abraham was called righteous by God because of his faith, not his obedience to the law. Abraham precedes the law which God gave to Moses. This study of Abrahamic righteousness, expounded upon by Enduring Word Bible Commentaries, clearly explains this Pauline position.

Just as Abraham "believed God, and it was accounted to him for righteousness."

a) **Just as Abraham**: Among the Galatian Christians, the push towards a works-based relationship with God came from certain other Christians who were born as Jews and who claimed Abraham as their spiritual ancestor. Therefore, Paul used **Abraham** as an example of being right before God by **faith** and not by faith plus works.

i. "It mattered a great deal to the apostle that God saves people by grace, not on the grounds of their human achievement, and he found Abraham an excellent example of that truth." (Morris)

b) **Abraham believed God, and it was accounted to him for righteousness**: Paul here quoted from Genesis 15:6. It simply shows that **righteousness** was **accounted** to Abraham because he **believed God**. It was *not* because he performed some work and certainly not because he was circumcised, because the covenant of circumcision had not yet been given.

   i.   Genesis 15:1-6 shows that when Abraham put his trust in God, specifically in God's promise to give him children that would eventually bring forth the Messiah, God credited this belief to Abraham's account as righteousness. "Abraham was not justified merely because he believed that God would multiply his seed, but because he embraced the grace of God, trusting to the promised Mediator." (Calvin)

   ii. There are essentially two types of righteousness: righteousness we *accomplish* by our own efforts and righteousness *accounted* to us by the work of God when we believe. Since none of us can be good enough to accomplish perfect righteousness, we must have God's righteousness accounted to us by doing just what Abram did: **Abraham believed God**.

c) **Abraham believed God, and it was accounted to him for righteousness**: This quotation from Genesis 15:6 is one of the clearest expressions in the Bible of the truth of salvation by grace, through faith alone. It is the gospel in the Old Testament, quoted four times in the New

Testament (Romans 4:3, Romans 4:9-10, Romans 4:22 and here in Galatians 3:6

   i.   Romans 4:9-10 makes much of the fact this righteousness was accounted to Abraham before he was *circumcised* (Genesis 17). No one could say Abraham was made righteous because of his obedience or fulfillment of religious law or ritual. It was faith and faith alone that caused God to account Abraham as righteous.

   ii. We should be careful to say that Abraham's faith did not make him righteous. Abraham's *God* made him righteous, by accounting his faith to him for righteousness. "His faith was not his righteousness, but God so rewarded his exercise of faith, as that upon it he reckoned (or imputed)...the righteousness of him in whom he believed." (Poole)

d) **Accounted to him for righteousness**: Abraham's experience shows that God *accounts* us as righteous, because of what Jesus did for us, as we receive what He did for us by faith. (https://enduringword.com/bible-commentary/galatians-3/#top)

Take that in - righteousness by faith preceded the righteousness by observance of the law. God had already established the path of righteousness by faith - God did that, not man. Man perverted the law which God gave by adding more and more laws, making it impossible to fully observe. God said we are justified by our faith. Wow.

The law carries with it a curse. Christ became that curse for us by taking on our sin and hanging on the cross in our place. Who wouldn't serve our God? What could possibly persuade you otherwise? He saw us through the annals of time and had a plan to justify us, save us, and call us righteous.

Amen.

Galatians 3:15 Brothers, let me take an example from everyday life. Just as no one can set aside or add to a human covenant that has been duly established, so it is in this case.

Galatians 3:16 Now to Abraham and his seed were the promises made. He saith not, And to seeds, as of many; but as of one, AND TO THY SEED, which is Christ.

Gentiles were to understand that it was not a blood tie of genetics that gave them this connection to Abraham, and therefore not the law. It is, by God's own words, the faith tie that connects even us to Abraham. The faith tie that assured us the connection to the seed - Jesus Christ. The actions of Jesus Christ opened the door to salvation and our faith unlocked that door. My Lord, who wouldn't love, worship, and serve you! We are heirs of this promise by our FAITH!

Reflection

Write a prayer of thanksgiving for our Abrahamic inheritance because of our FAITH.

_____

_____

_____

_____

_____

_____

_____

_____

_____

_____

_____

_____

Strength to the Inner Man

Ephesians 3:16

Ephesians 3:16 That he would grant you, according to the riches of his glory, to be strengthened with might by his Spirit in the inner man.

Knowing Who You Are

It would be easy to blow past the greetings of Paul's letter because they appear to be so formulaic. That would be a mistake because we need to clearly understand how Paul understands himself and how he wants the church to understand who they are. In other words, IDENTITY MATTERS. It is only when we know who we are that we are equipped with the confidence to move in our purpose, exercise our gifts, and manifest those things which have been ordained to our hands - IDENTITY MATTERS. Ephesians 1:1 Paul, an apostle of Jesus Christ by the will of God, to the saints which are at Ephesus, and to the faithful in Chris Jesus.

Three words jump out at me immediately: apostle, saints, and faithful. These are not new but I'm pressed to shine a light on specific words in this book of Ephesians because of the sheer magnitude of his message.

- **Apostle [652] apostolos** - an ambassador of the Gospel; officially a commissioner of Christ (with miraculous powers):- he that is sent.
- **Saints [40] hagios** - sacred [physically pure, morally blameless or religious, consecrated]:- holy.
- **Faithful [4103] pistos** - trustful:- believe(ing, r); sure, true

So, at the very outset he wants to establish in these believers exactly who he is and who they are: each one has been chosen by God for a specific reason. Paul has been called by God as a spokesperson for the Gospel, in essence its protector ensuring that it is clearly understood and not misrepresented. The people must come to accept and understand that they have been consecrated, even though they are surrounded by paganism and a variety of other beliefs and religious practices. They are called to be those who trust and are sure of the word that they have received about Jesus Christ.

Ephesians 1:3 Blessed be the God and Father of our Lord Jesus Christ, who hath blessed us with all spiritual blessings in heavenly places in Christ:

What is being said here is profound and probably overlooked. They are told that they are blessed with a blessing while being told that God is to be blessed by them.

Blessed [eulogetos] [2128] adorable,blessed be the God and Father of our Lord Jesus Christ, who hath blessed [eulogeo] [2127] to speak well of, to thank or invoke a benediction upon, prosper; praise us with all spiritual [pneumatikos] [4152] non-carnal, supernatural blessings [eulogia] [2129] elegance of language; commendations; consecration in heavenly places in Christ.

Our God, whom we are to bless by loving and adoring him, is speaking well of us, praying for us, and praising us with supernatural consecrations in heaven through the actions of Jesus Christ. How powerful a realization is that! Our Lord speaks highly of us in the presence of his father. We, like the Ephesians, are so precious in his sight that we have been adopted. So much so that he redeemed them and us with his own blood, forgiving their and our sins, that when the time is right we would all be gathered unto himself. We have an inheritance in him. IDENTITY MATTERS!

Ephesians 1:11 In whom also we have obtained an inheritance, being predestinated according to the purpose of him who worked all things after the counsel of his own will.

Ephesians 1:12 That we should be to the praise of his glory, who first trusted in Christ.

Ephesians 1:13 In whom ye also trusted, after that ye heard the word of truth, the gospel of your salvation: in whom also after that ye believed, ye were sealed with that holy Spirit of promise,

Ephesians 1:14 Which is the earnest of our inheritance until the redemption of the purchased possession, unto the praise of his glory.

Yes, we, like the Ephesians, have an inheritance of which we are already partly in possession - the earnestness of the promise. We received this earnestness of the promise immediately upon our acceptance and belief in the gospel. Because of that we have been sealed, we are secure in Christ Jesus by our being sealed with the Holy Spirit, the earnest of the promise. The Holy Spirit brings illumination of the word, guides and directs us, comforts us until that day when Christ shall return. The Holy Spirit is the earnestness of the promise [arrhabon] [728] pledge, part of the purchase, money or property, given in advance as security for the rest. On that great day we shall receive in full the promise from our Savior. Paul prayed that understanding would be granted of who they were and we are in Jesus.

Another part of this blessed identity is the fact that they had been quickened, that is made alive because of their faith and the power of the Holy Spirit which indwells believers. The reality that sin separates from God is a startling reality. This separation is likened unto death as sin causes sinners to go farther and farther away from God and his purpose for our lives.

Ephesians 2:1 And you hath he quickened, who were dead in trespasses and sins;

Ephesians 2:2 Wherein in time past ye walked according to the course of this world, according to the prince of the power of the air, the spirit that now worketh in the children of disobedience:

This passage is awesomely powerful because it affirms the fact that you do not have to remain in sin. No one needs to remain in a state that leads to spiritual death and a hellish earthly existence. The reality is that this is only existence and not life: sin is cyclical leading to the same patterns of spiritual and emotional poverty, degradation, humiliation, depression, and eventually death. This is on full display in many of our communities - they have died on the vine. What is the root cause? Sin. It runs rampant and free and individuals have come to believe that they are powerless to bring about change in any form. That is a lie! Change begins in the heart that seeks and finds Christ. That is when and where life begins anew.

Ephesians 2:4 But God, who is rich in mercy, for his great love wherewith he loved us,

Ephesians 2:5 Even when we were dead in sins, hath quickened us together with Christ, (by grace ye are saved;)

I'm reminded of the song "Love Lifted Me". It says when nothing else could help, love lifted me. And God's love can go as far down as it needs to reach anyone and will lift us from the dead places in our lives to places we didn't even know existed. He, with his love, will lift us when we didn't even believe we were worthy. He will lift us when we thought it couldn't be done.

Yes He will. Yes His Love will! Just believe He will and he will.

Ephesians 2:8 For by grace ye are saved through faith; and that not of yourselves: it is the gift of God:

Ephesians 2:9 Not of works, lest any man should boast.

You do not have to do anything more than have the faith to believe who Jesus is and God showers you with grace, freely, to be entirely new. We have been ordained, that is set apart, to do good works. We are to live our lives walking in these good works, that is doing them. God looked at all men and presented the same grace through the actions of his son Jesus. There is no separation, not even that which was erected because of the traditions and beliefs of men. There is no circumcision and uncircumcision because faith has closed that chasm.

Ephesians 2:11 Wherefore remember, that you being in the past Gentiles in the flesh, who are called Uncircumcision by that which is called the
Circumcision in the flesh made by hands;

Ephesians 2:12 That at that time ye were without Christ, being aliens from the commonwealth of Israel, and strangers from the covenants of promise, having no hope, and without God in the worlds:

Ephesians 2:13 But now in Christ Jesus ye who sometimes were far off are made nigh by the blood of Christ.

Ephesians 2:14 For he is our peace, who hath made both one, and hath broken down the middle wall of partition between us;

Because of what Christ did on Calvary, his obedience unto death, there was no more reason for anyone to be separate from God. There were no more reasons for some to have access and others not to - the veil was torn in two and all could access salvation. Salvation became free to all, not because of the Law, not because of works, but because of faith in Jesus Christ. That truth remains so no one needs to think that they need to work on themselves before they are ready to come to Christ. Believe and come.

That is all.

Ephesians 2:19 Now therefore ye are no more strangers and foreigners, but fellow citizens with the saints, and of the household of God; Ephesians 2:20 And are built upon the foundation of the apostles and prophets, Jesus Christ himself being the chief cornerstone;

Ephesians 2:21 In whom all the building fitly framed together groweth unto an holy temple in the Lord:

Ephesians 2:22 In whom ye also are builded together for an habitation of God through the Spirit.

Full access is for everyone to be the temple of the Living God. This was the calling of Paul's life - to share this miraculous reality with those who were not Jewish born, the Gentiles. Up until this revelation the focus had been primarily on converting the Jews to belief in Jesus Christ as he was the fulfillment of all the prophecies of the Messiah. They believed it was their blood born inheritance and only to them but the Apostle Paul has delivered the message to everyone, not just the Jews in the far reaches of the known world but to everyone who would receive this gospel and believe. We are also beneficiaries of this grace.

Ephesians 3:6 That the Gentiles should be fellow heirs, and of the same body, and partakers of his promise in Christ by the gospel:

Ephesians 3:13 Wherefore I desire that ye faint not at my tribulations for you, which is your glory.

Ephesians 3:14 For this cause I bow my knees unto the Father of our Lord Jesus Christ,

Ephesians 3:15 Of whom the whole family in heaven and earth is named, **Ephesians 3:16 That he would grant you, according to the riches of his glory, to be strengthened with might by his Spirit in the inner man;**

Paul had been through so much to preach this unadulterated gospel to the Gentiles and here he encouraged them that they were not concerned for him. He wants them to continue in the faith and be strengthened in their inner man. What is this inner man of which he began to speak? Literally, he means what's on the inside of a human. And what is there? The Holy Spirit who indwells believers. The love and grace of God which he so freely gave. The love of Christ which redeemed , justified, and sanctified all believers. The word, that living word which should be the treasure of our hearts. Those things should be in the inner man and should be growing with each breath we take by the power of the Holy Spirit of God.

Reflection

What was Paul's core message to the church at Ephesus? Does that message resonate in your spirit?

_____

_____

_____

_____

_____

_____

_____

_____

_____

_____

_____

_____

Let Us Mind the Same Thing

Philippians 3:16

Philippians 3:16 Nevertheless, whereto we have already attained, let us walk by the same rule, let us mind the same thing.

The Servant's Heart and Mind

This is a very personal and affectionate letter from Paul to the church at Philippi. He, Timotheus, and Epaphroditus had an undeniable love for this church as they had for them. This is displayed in the language and nurture that pours through the pages of this brief letter. Modern congregations long to be loved in this same way but for some that is not the relationship they have with their pastors and other church leaders. Church hurts are real but all hurts, no matter how deep, can be loved out of a congregation. They can be loved to life and learn to love and trust one another as a body of Christ.

Philippians 1:9 And this I pray, that your love may abound yet more and more in knowledge and in all judgment;

Philippians 1:10 That ye may approve things that are excellent; that ye me be sincere and without offense till the day of Christ;

Philippians 1:11 Being filled with the fruits of righteousness, which are by Jesus Christ, unto the glory and praise of God.

The 3:16 Challenge

Remembering this congregation brought Paul joy, especially during his time under house arrest for preaching the gospel. He was very confident that this church would continue to grow and prosper even while he was imprisoned for various reasons among which was the fact that they had sent charitable gifts to him during his imprisonment. These gifts allowed his ministry to continue even while he was in bonds. Paul took comfort in the fact that the gospel was still being preached even though not all those who claimed to be sincere in that office were; there were still others who preached with fervor and zeal for the cause of Christ.

Philippines 1:14 And many of the brethren in the Lord, waxing confident by my bonds, are much more bold to speak the word without fear.

Philippians 1:15 Some indeed preach Christ even of envy and strife; and some also of good will:

Philippians 1:16 The one preach Christ of contention, not sincerely, supposing to add affliction to my bonds:

Philippians 1:17 But the other of love, knowing that I am set for the defense of the gospel.

Philippians 1:18 What then? Notwithstanding, every way, whether in pretense, or in truth, Christ is preached; and I therein do rejoice, yea, and will rejoice.

The purpose and calling of his life had so focused him on Christ that even those dire circumstances could not deter him. His mind was so set on the ministry to the Gentiles that he could not be bothered by those who had the wrong intent - the word was still going forth. The fact that his very life was in the balance did not bother him. Listen to his bold declaration -

Philippians 1:21 For me to live is Christ, and to die is gain.

By living he would continue to preach the gospel of Jesus Christ, winning more believers for the Lord. Yet, to die he would be in the presence of God Almighty and gain what his faith had promised him - eternity in glory. Either way he would rejoice. His great earthly joy would be that the church would continue in unity and fellowship.

Philippians 2:1 If there be therefore any consolation in Christ, if any comfort of love, if any fellowship of the Spirit, if any bowels and mercies, Philippians 2:2 Fulfill ye my joy, that ye be like-minded, having the same love, being of one accord, of one mind.

Philippians 2:6 Who, being in the form of God, thought it not robbery to be equal with God:

Philippians 2:5 Let this mind be in you, which was also in Christ Jesus:

Philippians 2:7 But made himself of no reputation, and took upon him the form of a servant, and was made in likeness of men:

Philippians 2:8 And being found in fashion as a man, he humbled himself, and became obedient unto death, even the death of the cross.

These oft quoted scriptures are seldom clearly understood. What is the heart of these verses? God the Father, God the Son, and God the Holy Spirit are equal being the Godhead, They are three distinct persons yet one God - the Trinity. Therefore it was not robbery for Jesus to consider himself equal with God. He teaches us saying "I and my Father are one." What's amazing is the choice he makes to become man; to be humbled, humiliated, obedient, denigrate, to suffer, and to die. He knew all of that was coming and willingly accepted it - he made up his mind to do that for us. Do you have the mind to do that? This is the magnitude of what Paul is saying to them and us. Do we have the mind of Christ? Can we love like that?

That is an extremely tall order and to help them he sends Epaphroditus, whom they clearly have a relationship with and whom they love in the Lord. Timotheus was to be sent later. Both men were sent to edify the church and to be edified by them. Epaphroditus had been very ill, to the point of death, they knew that and were concerned. You know how it is when someone you love has something hard happen - you want to see them and they want to see you.

Philippians 2:26 For he longed after you all, and was full of heaviness, because that ye had heard that he had been sick.

Philippians 2:27 For indeed he was sick nigh unto death: but God had mercy on him; and not on him only, but on me also, lest I should have sorrow upon sorrow.

Philippians 2:28 I sent him therefore the more carefully, that, when ye see him again, ye may rejoice, and that I may be less sorrowful.

Here we are granted a look at the power of fellowship within ministry. Love is obvious among them, the love of the Lord. I pray that every fellowship has this kind of love and genuine concern for each other, more than just for the work of the ministry but for the humanity of each other. That we take the time to love one another, nurture one another, edify one another, check on one another. Simple yet sincere gestures that mirror the heart of our Lord.

If we don't have love for one another then what is the point? If we don't love the Lord then why pursue this kind of life? With all that Paul had, the reputation, the esteem of his peers, the strength of his lineage - he willingly walked away from all of it to fulfill the call to preach the gospel to the Gentiles.

Philippians 3:8 Yea doubtless, and I count all things but loss for the excellency of the knowledge of Christ Jesus my Lord: for whom I have suffered the loss of all things, and do count them but dung, that I may win Christ,

Philippians 3:9 And be found in him, not having mine own righteousness, which is of the law, but that which is through the faith of Christ, the righteousness which is of God by faith:

Philippians 3:10 That I may know him, and the power of his resurrection, and the fellowship of his sufferings, being made conformable unto his death;

Is there anything, absolutely anything, that you would prefer to have more than Jesus Christ? Is there any part of your life that has not been made better because of Christ? Is there anywhere that you would long to go where you couldn't bring Jesus? There isn't one thing in my life that I esteem higher than Christ. Without him what do I need any of these things for? Where would I need to go where Jesus can't go? Who would I even be without Christ? No one I would care to know...that's for sure. I relate to Paul. He is a God chaser. He might be one of the first "Jesus Freaks." He saw very clearly what mattered, not just in his own personal life but he saw how God could use his life to impact the world. My Lord. Can you see how God could use you to impact the world? What you were is irrelevant - it's who you're going to be in Christ that matters.

Philippians 3:13 Brethren, I count not myself to have apprehended: but this one thing I do, forgetting those things which are behind, and reaching forth unto those things which are before,

Philippians 3:14 I press toward the mark for the prize of the high calling of God in Christ Jesus.

Philippians 3:15 Let us therefore, as many as be perfect, be thus minded: and if anything ye be otherwise minded, God shall reveal even this unto you.

Philippians 3:16 Nevertheless, whereto we have already attained, let us walk by the same rule, let us mind the same thing.

Paul is telling us that he is not yet fully mature, that he still has room to grow and goals to reach for in God. Those things that are behind him, every bit of his past, the good, the bad, and the ugly those things are all done. There is still much to do. He was going to continue to make every effort to do those things which were ordained for his hands - those things God had for him to do. He called for those who were mature to do the same things - do what God has for you to do. Leave the past where it is and move forward in the Lord. Every believer should aim to achieve those things that God has for them - what God has for you is most definitely for you. The collective goals of the body of Christ are to win others to Christ and to be faithful servants of him. Obedience, humility, and love - those are the rules by which we live, like-mindedness with Christ.

Reflection

Examine your life walk, what do you need to bring in line with the mind of Christ?

_____

_____

_____

_____

_____

_____

_____

_____

_____

_____

_____

_____

Let the Word of Christ Dwell in You Richly

Colossians 3:16

Colossians 3:16 Let the word of Christ dwell in you richly in all wisdom; teaching and admonishing one another in psalms and hymns and spiritual songs, singing with grace in your hearts to the Lord.

Bearing the Fruit of the Gospel

I have been fortunate to witness the births of several ministries and can attest that it ain't easy. There tends to be the pull towards the familiar even when attempting to bring forth that which is new. We rally around those things which are familiar, they are comforting, they don't stretch us, don't require or insist upon reflection, they simply are mechanically engaged in. That dilemma is not a new dilemma. The church at Colosse, under the leadership of Epaphras, was in such a situation. Now it was not Epaphras who was bringing back the old familiar habits, it was other teachers who were intent upon mixing the Gospel with pagan ideals and ritualistic practices. Epaphras knew he needed the help of Paul. It was not that they lacked the love of Christ they needed to grow in their understanding of the preeminence of Christ and walk in that which they had been taught of him. Paul wrote this letter, like so many of the others, from the bonds of prison and with the same enthusiasm for the believers. He expressed his love for them and gratitude for them and quickly addressed the heart of the issue - false teachings.

Colossians 1:3 We give thanks to God and the Father of our Lord Jesus Christ, praying always for you,

Colossians 1:4 Since we heard of your faith in Christ Jesus, and the love which you have to all saints,

Colossians 1:5 For the hope which is laid up for you in heaven, whereof ye heard before in the word of the truth of the gospel:

Colossians 1:6 Which is come unto you, as it is in all the world; and bringeth forth fruit, as it doth also in you, since the day ye heard of it, and knew the grace of God in truth:

Colossians 1:7 As ye also learned of Epaphras our dear fellow servant, who is for you a faithful minister of Christ;

Colossians 1:8 Who also declared unto us your love in the Spirit.

Right at the outset Paul declares the good that is in this church at Colosse: their love, that they have received the word of truth, that they have sound leadership who loves them, that they are faithful - these are powerful affirming declarations to this body. Yet he goes on to exhort them, assuring them that he is praying for them, specifically that they "be filled with knowledge of his will in all wisdom and spiritual understanding" (Col. 1:9). He further alludes to the fact that these points of growth would cause them to "walk worthy of the Lord unto all pleasing, being fruitful in every good work, and increasing in the knowledge of God;" (Col. 1:10). These points of spiritual growth should be the heart's desire of every church leader for the body of Christ. To know Jesus on an intimate level and to minister to the needs, big or small, of all of God's people. These actions are done out of gratitude to God who, through his Son, redeemed man from his sin through his shed blood. This Jesus has got to be clearly understood as the sole source of redemption and that he alone is worthy of our worship. Paul sets out to firmly establish these points in their hearts, minds, and spirits.

Colossians 1:12 Giving thanks unto the Father, which hath made us meet to be partakers of the inheritance of the saints in light:

Colossians 1:13 Who hath delivered us from the power of darkness, and hath translated us into the kingdom of his dear Son:

Colossians 1:14 In whom we have redemption through his blood, even forgiveness of sins:

This is what Jesus Christ has done by his blood!

Colossians 1:15 Who is the image of the invisible God, the firstborn of every creature:

This is who Jesus Christ is!

Colossians 1:16 For by him were all things created, that are in heaven, and that are in earth, visible and invisible, whether they be thrones, or dominions, or principalities. or powers: all things were created by him, and for him:
Colossians 1:17 And he is before all things, and by him all things consist.

This is who Jesus Christ is by his creative omnipotence.

Colossians 1:18 And he is the head of the body, the church: who is the beginning, the firstborn from the dead; that in all things he might have the preeminence.
Colossians 1:19 For it pleased the Father that in him should all fulness dwell;

This is why Jesus Christ, and this name alone, is worthy of and due our worship!

Because of the shedding of the blood of Jesus Christ, Paul reiterates for them afresh, sins are forgiven, you are blameless, you are reconciled, and justified. Faith in the gospel assures this for every believer. Paul longed to come to them, for he had not ministered to them in person, and he also desired that this letter be read to the church at Laodicea. Both of these churches were in Asia Minor, near modern day Turkey. We prayed that those within these congregations continued to walk in love and grew in the assurances of understanding of the mysteries of God. We presented a warning to both churches as well.

Colossians 2:6 As ye therefore received Christ Jesus the Lord, so walk in him:
Colossians 2:7 Rooted and built up in him, and stablished in the faith, as ye have been taught, abounding therein with thanksgiving.

Colossians 2:8 Beware lest any man spoil you through philosophy and vain deceit, after the tradition of men, after the rudiments of the world, and not after Christ.

This word of warning is absolutely relevant today. We must hold on to what we've been taught and studied about the savior. It must be hidden as a treasure in our hearts so that we do not succumb to sin or deceit. We must, as I tell my students, "KNOW WHAT WE KNOW!" Once that word of truth is settled in your heart, hold on to it. That's the word of truth though, that can be found in the bible, not just what somebody said. You've got to be able to confirm that what you're standing on is God's word. Many people have come and persuaded many more and they have been standing on their own doctrines, precepts, and assertions - not God's word. Be sure, be very sure that your foundation is the WORD OF GOD!

What did this word do for the Gentile churches? It afforded them both salvation and redemption through their faith; they were called righteous because they believed God just as Abraham was called righteous by God because he believed God. They were not under the law, did not need to be circumcised in the flesh - their circumcision was spiritual, as is ours. We have cut away the desires of the flesh that led us away from God our Father and toward a life of sin. They were no longer under the condemnation of the Law or any other man made precepts or ordinances.

Colossians 2:16 Let no man therefore judge you in meat, or in drink, or in respect of an holiday, or of the new moon, or of the sabbath days: Colossians 2:17 Which are a shadow of things to come; but the body is of Christ.

These newborns in Christ were being confronted by Judaizers, Jews who wanted them to convert to Judaism and observe the Law before converting to Christianity, and by pagans who had beliefs of all sorts that they were trying to infiltrate into the body of believers. They needed to be crystal clear on how their salvation and redemption had been given - it had nothing to do with works or things that could be done to the flesh. It was solely a matter of belief that granted salvation, baptism in the Holy Spirit, redemption from the eternal penalty of sin, and an eternal life with Jesus Christ. That being said now they had to shift their focus from earthly carnal things to heavenly spiritual things.

Colossians 3:1 If ye be risen with Christ, seek those things which are above, where Christ sitteth on the right hand of God.

Colossians 3:2 Set your affections on things above, not on things on the earth.

Colossians 3:3 For ye are dead, and your life is hid with Christ in God. Colossians 3:4 When Christ, who is our life, shall appear, then shall ye also appear with him in glory.

This is the necessary change that must take place in the lives of every believer. That inner man, that longed after the things of the flesh, must be put under subjection. What does that look like? Say "NO" to those things that you used to run to for pleasure. Seek after the things of God. Become a God Chaser. Seek to know his ways. Seek to apply the word to your life.

Seek to live a life which glorifies God and does not shame him.

Colossians 3:12 Put on therefore, as he elect of God, holy and beloved, bowels of mercies, kindness, humbleness of mind, meekness, longsuffering;

Colossians 3:13 Forbearing one another, and forgiving one another, if any man have a quarrel against any: even as Christ forgave you, so also do ye. Colossians 3:14 And above all these things put on charity, which is the bond of perfectness.

Colossians 3:15 And let the peace of God rule in your hearts, to which also ye are called in one body; and be ye thankful.

Colossians 3:16 Let the word of Christ dwell in you richly in all wisdom; teaching and admonishing one another in psalms and hymns and spiritual songs, singing with grace in your hearts to the Lord.

How can we let the word of Christ dwell in us richly? Come to know it through study, prayer, and meditation. Certainly a word that is not in you can not dwell richly, right? The richness comes by the diligence of prayer and study as the Holy Spirit illuminates God's word before you. We are told to ask God if there are things in his word which we do not understand. We are further told that he will give us understanding - withholding nothing. And this word is rich! As we come to know better and to make applications in our lives through the wisdom of the word the manifestation of the promises begin to fill your life. Allow it to dwell in you richly. With the richness of this word you are able to discern the attacks of the adversary and deflect and defeat them. With the richness of this word you are able to lead others to salvation in Jesus Christ. With the richness of this word your faith will grow, as will your power, your boldness. Let this word dwell richly in you!

Reflection

What parallels can you see between your walk in Christ and that of the Colossians? What are your points of growth?

_____

_____

_____

_____

_____

_____

_____

_____

_____

_____

_____

_____

_____

The Lord of Peace

II Thessalonians 3:16

II Thessalonians 3:16 Now the Lord of peace himself give you peace always by all means. The Lord be with you all.

Assurances in the Faith

The second letter to the Thessalonians comes from Paul, Silvanus, and Timotheus as a source of comfort to the believers in that church. They are assured that their righteousness in the sight of God guarantees that they will have to endure some tribulations. We must realize this as well though some newborn believers erroneously believe that by giving their lives to Christ all will suddenly be rainbows and lollipops. That is not the case. Once you openly declare that you are on the Lord's side...tribulations will come. The stronger you are in Christ the more your adversary will attack but the more grace you will receive to endure and overcome.

II Thessalonians 1:4 So that we ourselves glory in you in the churches of God for your patience and faith in all your persecutions and tribulations that ye endure:

II Thessalonians 1:5 Which is a manifest token of the righteous judgment of God, that ye may be counted worthy of the kingdom of God, for which ye also suffer:

We are taking on the likeness and mind of Christ. It should be expected that we will suffer in a similar manner also. If Christ suffered then why not me? Why not us? However those who have been used to bring us suffering will be made to suffer on that glorious day when Christ returns again in the clouds with his angels.

II Thessalonians 1:7 And to you who are troubled rest with us, when the

Lord Jesus shall be revealed from heaven with his mighty angels, II Thessalonians 1:8 In flaming fire taking vengeance on them that know not God, and that obey not the gospel of our Lord Jesus Christ:

II Thessalonians 1:9 Who shall be punished with everlasting destruction from the presence of the Lord, and from the glory of his power;

Too often we feel overwhelmed by the attacks that the adversary mounts against us but just absorb what is being said here. Those who have been used to torment the believers, my Lord, the penalty for them is far worse than anything they could ever hurl at us. My prayer for those who attack believers is that the scales would fall from their eyes and that they repent while they yet have time. Should they choose not to repent their eternity is sure. But to the saints, prayers that they would continue to be counted worthy of their calling by God. That is my prayer as well.

The heart of the issue for the Thessalonian church is a grievous teaching that had apparently been spread and caused significant upset in the church. Not only did it go against what they had been taught but it was an intentional deception of God's people. What was this lie? It was that the Day of the Lord, the prophesied return, had already occurred.

II Thessalonians 2:1 Now we beseech you, brethren, by the coming of our

Lord Jesus Christ, and by our gathering together unto him,

II Thessalonians 2:2 That ye be not soon shaken in mind, or be troubled, neither by spirit, nor by word, nor by letter as from us, as that the day of Christ is at hand.

Someone had gone so far as to forge a letter to make it appear as though it had come from Paul with this heinous lie. He soon stamps out this forgery and goes about to reassure the church that they have not missed the coming again of the Savior. So he reminds them of those things which they have been taught, in particular what will precede the coming of the Lord. II Thessalonians 2:3 Let no man deceive you by any means: for that day shall not come, except there come a falling away first, and that man of sin be revealed, the son of perdition;

II Thessalonians 2:4 Who opposeth and exalteth himself above all that is called God, or that is worshipped; so that he as God sitteth in the temple of God, shewing himself that he is God.

II Thessalonians 2:5 Remember ye not, that, when I was yet with you, I told you these things?

The church should not have been shaken by the letter or teachings that caused this stir. Why? They had already been taught and should have known better - their discernment should have kicked in. But, unfortunately, they were shaken almost to the core by a lie. However Paul is careful to have them recall the prophetic scriptures which he had presented to them from the book of Daniel. These scriptures would have been well known to Jews and Jewish converts but would have been unfamiliar to Gentiles. That could have been partly the reason that they did not call out the lies and liars in their midst. This further reveals the necessity of teaching as a vital part of ministry. Teachers must be equipped to teach God's people so that they will not be deceived and led astray by any message that sounds the least bit persuasive. By the same token the people must be in place to receive the instruction and to apply the discipline of study for themselves. No one should be satisfied with "introductory level" knowledge of God. Little knowledge - little power. Much knowledge - much power. Those who willfully deceive the church will face the wrath of almighty God.

And after this very strong and pointed instruction comes a request for prayer for deliverance from those who are not faithful and a charge of strong discipline, admonishing the church to follow the commands which were written in the letter. "And we have confidence in the Lord touching you, that ye both do and will do the things which we command you"(I Thess. 2:4). The instructions are very specific and seem to allude to the fact that someone, or possibly several individuals, had tried to take advantage of the charitable goodness of the saints - they refused to work. Their refusal to work was apparently validated, at least in their own minds, by the comparison between themselves and the apostle and his fellow ministers.

II Thessalonians 3:6 Now we command you, brethren, in the name of our Lord Jesus Christ, that ye withdraw yourselves from every brother that walketh disorderly, and not after the tradition which he received of us. II Thessalonians 3:7 For yourselves know how ye ought follow us: for we behaved not ourselves disorderly among you;

II Thessalonians 3:8 Neither did we eat any man's bread for nought; but wrought with labour and travail night and day, that we might not be chargeable to any of you:

II Thessalonians 3:9 Not because we have not power, but to make ourselves an ensample unto you to follow us.

II Thessalonnians 3:10 For even when we were with you, this we commanded you, that if any would not work, neither should he eat. Ii Thessalonians 3:11 For we hear that there are some who walk among you disorderly, working not at all, but are busybodies.

These verses are rather practical for those in ministry and for those being ministered unto - they speak to work ethic and integrity. Paul has the church to recall what they experienced with him, Silvanus, and Timotheus. These three ministers did not come to Thessalonica and live off of the church - they worked. They had no intention of being a burden - chargeable [1912] [epibareo] expensive to or heavy upon the church. Therefore they worked day and night. Now he points out that this was not because they did not have power - [1849] [exousia] privilege, influence, or authority that could have warranted such treatment, being well taken care of that is. But they wanted to be an ensample - [5179] [tupos] a die, stamp, resemblance after which they, the church, could model their own behavior. So what should have been gleaned from their example? If you don't work you do not eat. That is one of the mantras of our household - we all pull our own weight so that we do not become burdensome to everyone else. Surely the church should do no less and expect no less.

To the contrary, there were folks in the midst of the Thessalonian church who were determined to do nothing and cause problems. You already know where I'm going with this don't you? Every congregation everywhere can relate to this scenario...but we don't want to. Now, for many of these individuals their lack of work within the body is sheer laziness, preferring to sit back and complain or find fault with the work that is being done by those who are willingly doing it. He calls them "busybodies" and that term has garnered the connotation of some harmless though aggravating talkers. Paul is indicating an individual who is far more dangerous than harmless. Busybodies - [4020] peri ergazomai - to work all around, bustle about, and meddle are way more industrious than they would have you to believe. Their grubby little hands are in all the places where they shouldn't be, along with their ears and their mouths. They stir the pot, if you will, then sit back to watch it burn. They are disorderly - [814] [ataktos] - unruly and religiously insubordinate. Even within the Greek word you can see the root word for attack and that is what they do and Paul commands them to withdraw themselves from everyone who behaves in this way. If they are not following the example that they presented and walked out in their presence and exhort or encourage them "by our Lord Jesus Christ, that with quietness they work, and eat their own bread" (II Thess. 3:12). True words of wisdom teaching us today from antiquity. And with final words of instruction he then offers his closing salutation.

II Thessalonians 3:13 But ye, brethren, be not weary in well doing. II Thessalonians 3:14 And if any man obey not our word by this epistle, note that man, and have no company with him, that he may be ashamed. II Thessalonians 3:15 Yet count him not as an enemy, but admonish him as a brother.

II Thessalonians 3:16 Now the Lord of peace himself give you peace always by all means. The Lord be with you all.

What an apropos closing to this letter. The commands were harsh. The instruction was necessary. The closing, loving and nurturing. This is what ministry should be - a reflection of Jesus Christ in every sense.

Reflection

How can Paul's instructions and commands to the Thessalonian church be enacted in the contemporary church? Do you think this kind of instruction would be well received today?

_____

_____

_____

_____

_____

_____

_____

_____

_____

_____

_____

_____

_____

The Mystery of Godliness

I Timothy 3:16

I Timothy 3:16 And without controversy great is the mystery of godliness: God was manifest in the flesh, justified in the Spirit, seen of angels, preached unto the Gentiles, believed on in the world, received up into glory.

Instructions: Father to Son in Ministry

The Pauline epistles which we've studied thus far have each been written to churches. Here is something different - an epistle to a pastor whom Paul personally converted to Christianity and whom he loves as a son, Timothy. This young man is also unique in that he was both Jewish and Greek; having experience in both worlds he was supremely qualified to lead the Ephesian church. This was a young church and Timothy was a young pastor. He was in a society that was pagan culturally and was learning what Christianity was and how life was transformed by these new beliefs. In other words there were challenges.

I Timothy 1:3 As I besought thee to abide still at Ephesus, when I went to Macedonia, that thou mightest charge some that they teach no other doctrine,

I Timothy 1:4 Neither give heed to fables and endless genealogies, which minister questions, rather than godly edifying which is in faith: so do.

Paul's concern was genuine, these people were in need of sound doctrine if the church was to stand those birth pangs and all the challenges which were yet to come. He is told to charge some to be charitable out of a pure heart and good conscience, and to have unfeigned faith (I Tim. 1:5). This was not due to any lack in Timothy but in those who sought to lead in the church at Ephesus.

I Timothy 1:6 From which some having swerved have turned aside unto vain jangling;

I Timothy 1:7 Desiring to be teachers of the law; understanding neither what they say, nor whereof they affirm.

Keep in mind that this is a pagan community who had been reminded that their righteousness did not come from the law but from the faith tied to Abraham. Abraham's faith was counted as righteousness by God and it was this same faith, believing in God, that gave the Gentiles the gift of salvation through the belief in Jesus Christ. This was the truth that was to be preached and taught although some were teaching the law. They had no true understanding of the law, as Paul so eloquently points out, so they were mishandling it. They misunderstood the principle of grace and were putting themselves, and those they taught, under the curse of the law.

I Timothy 1:8 But we know that the law is good, if a man use it lawfully; I Timothy 1:9 Knowing this, that the law is not made for a righteous man, but for the lawless and disobedient , for the ungodly and for sinners, for unholy and profane, for murderers of fathers and murderers of mothers, for manslayers,

I Timothy 1:10 For whoremongers, for them that defile themselves with mankind, for menstealers, for liars, for perjured persons, and if there be any other thing that is contrary to sound doctrine.

It is truly a dangerous thing for people to, as my grandmother would say, "Go off half-cocked." Meaning going off and being clueless, either partially or totally, and talking like they know something. It just never goes well. How much more dangerous for the church! Timothy was to be on guard against these kinds of things for the good of the saints.

I Timothy 1:18 This charge I commit unto thee, son Timothy, according to the prophecies which went before thee, that thou by them mightest war a good warfare;

I Timothy 1:19 Holding faith, an a good conscience; which some having put away concerning faith have made shipwreck:

I Timothy 1:20 Of whom is Hymenaeus and Alexander; whom I have delivered unto Satan, that they may learn not to blaspheme.

This last verse seems harsh but must speak to a work that was done against which they had been warned. After much prayer, I can only imagine, did Paul render such harsh words against these two. One can only hope that they did repent. And it is in the vain of prayer and supplication for leaders that Paul continues to write to Timothy. Why is it that we pray for those who are leaders, so that they may lead in a way that pleases God?

I Timothy 2:2 For kings, and for all that are in authority; that we may lead a quiet and peaceable life in all godliness and honesty.

I Timothy 2:3 For this is good and acceptable in the sight of God our Saviour;

I Timothy 2:4 Who will have all men to be saved, and come unto the knowledge of the truth.

I Timothy 2:5 For there is one God, and one mediator between God and men, the man Christ Jesus.

I Timothy 2:6 Who gave himself a ransom for all, to be testified in due time.

The purpose here is clear - to reiterate God's desire that all men should be saved. Therefore we pray for everyone, especially those who lead. Their decisions affect everyone else and God's hand is on the leaders and their power to lead. In ancient times politics and religion were tethered together. Decisions made by leaders were impactful in every aspect of people's lives. This is why Paul is so adamant in stressing this point to Timothy and in giving him further instruction in choosing the leadership of the church.

"Whereunto I am ordained a preacher, and an apostle, (I speak the truth in

Christ, and lie not;) a teacher of the Gentiles in faith and verity" (I Tim. 2:7). Paul wants so much for this word to go forth in purity, untarnished by anything that would prevent it from being received by God's people.

To this church, dropped in the midst of a pagan culture, there are more specific instructions. Here it is crucial that we understand the instructions in the context of the day in which they were given. These scriptures have been pulled out of context and have impacted congregations tremendously over the course of time. For clarity's sake, the Enduring Word Bible Commentary further illuminates Paul's perspectives on these issues. They are a reflection of both historical and cultural traditions which may not be broadly applied in contemporary culture.

A. Men and women in the church.

1. (8) The role of men in leading prayer when the church gathers.

I desire therefore that the men pray everywhere, lifting up holy hands, without wrath and doubting.

a) **That the men pray everywhere**: This has the idea of "In every church," and not of "In every place." Paul's focus is on what the church does when it comes together for meetings.

  i. The idea that we should pray constantly and that prayer should be a normal part of our lives wherever we go is good and valid; but it is not what Paul means here.

  ii. White on **everywhere**: "The directions are to apply to every Church without exception; no allowance is to be made for the conditions peculiar to any locality."

b) **That the men**: Makes it clear Paul assumed **men** would take the lead at meetings of the congregation. Since the lifting up of hands was a common posture of prayer in ancient cultures, this text speaks of men leading public prayer – men representing the congregation before God's throne.

  i. White translates the idea of the text: "The ministers of public prayer must be the men of the congregation, not the women."

c) **Lifting up holy hands**: Hands that are lifted up must be **holy** – hands that are set apart unto God, and not given over to evil.

d) **Without wrath and doubting**: Such prayers must be **without wrath** (praying "angry" prayers) and without **doubting** (praying without faith). When we pray angry, or pray without faith, we can do more bad than good – especially when the prayer is public.

i. "Having no vindictive feeling against any person; harboring no unforgiving spirit, while they are imploring pardon for their own offences." (Clarke)

2. (9-10) Women should emphasize *spiritual* preparation and beauty more than *physical* preparation and beauty.

In like manner also, that the women adorn themselves in modest apparel, with propriety and moderation, not with braided hair or gold or pearls or costly clothing, but, which is proper for women professing godliness, with good works.

a) **In like manner also**: The word **also** refers back to the statement *that the men pray everywhere* in 1 Timothy 2:8. Paul thought the principle of 1 Timothy 2:8 should apply in various congregations, and so should the principle in 1 Timothy 2:9.

b) **That the women adorn themselves in modest apparel**: This is how Christian women are supposed to dress, especially at their Christian meetings. The words **propriety and moderation** help explain what **modest apparel** is.

i. **Propriety** asks, "Is it appropriate for the occasion? Is it over-dressed or under-dressed? Is it going to call inappropriate attention to myself?" **Moderation** asks, "Is it moderate? Is it just too much – or far too little?" **Moderation** looks for a middle ground.

ii. The **braided hair or gold or pearls or costly clothing** Paul mentions were adornments that went against the principles of **propriety** and **moderation** in that culture.

iii. How you dress reflects your heart. If a man dresses in a casual manner, it says something about his attitude. Likewise, if a woman dresses in an immodest manner, it says something about her heart.

iv. "Woman has been invidiously defined: *An animal fond of dress.* How long will they permit themselves to be thus degraded?" (Clarke)

c) **But… with good works**: The most important adornment is **good works**. If a woman is dressed in propriety and moderation, with good works, she is perfectly dressed. **Good works** make a woman more beautiful than good jewelry.

3. (11-12) Women are to show submission, and yield to the authority of the men God has appointed to lead in the church.

Let a woman learn in silence with all submission. And I do not permit a woman to teach or to have authority over a man, but to be in silence.

a) **Let a woman learn in silence**: This unfortunate translation has led some to believe that it is forbidden for women to even speak in church meetings. Paul uses the same word translated **silence** in 1 Timothy 2:2, and it is translated *peaceable* there. The idea is *without contention* instead of total silence.

   i.   In other places in the New Testament, even in the writings of Paul, women are specifically mentioned as praying and speaking in the church (1 Corinthians 11:5). To **learn in silence** has the idea of women receiving the teaching of the men God has chosen to lead in the church, with **submission** instead of *contention*. ii. **Submission** is the principle; to **learn in silence** describes the application of the principle.

   ii. Some have said the reason for this is because in these ancient cultures (as well as some present-day cultures), men and women sat in separate sections. The thought is that women interrupted the church service by shouting questions and comments to their husbands during the service. Clarke expresses this idea: "It was lawful for *men* in public assemblies to ask questions, or even interrupt the speaker when there was any matter in his speech which they did not understand; but this liberty was not granted to *women*."

b) **With all submission**: The word for **submission** here literally means, "To be under in rank." It has to do with respecting an acknowledged order of authority. It certainly does not mean that men are more spiritual than women or that women are inferior to men.

   i.   "Anyone who has served in the armed forces knows that 'rank' has to do with order and authority, not with value or ability… Just as an army would be in confusion if there were no levels of authority, so society would be in chaos without submission." (Wiersbe)

c) **I do not permit a woman to teach or to have authority over a man**: Paul's meaning seems clear. Women are not to have the role of teaching authority in the church. To be *under authority* is the principle; *not teaching* is the application.

   i. Paul is saying that the church should not recognize women as those having authority in the church regarding matters of doctrine and Scriptural interpretation.

   ii. Not all speaking or teaching by a woman is *necessarily* a violation of God's order of authority in the church. Whatever speaking or teaching is done by a woman must be done in submission to the men God has appointed to lead the church.

   iii. 1 Corinthians 11:1-12 emphasizes the same principle. Women are to always act *under authority* in the congregation, demonstrated in Corinthian culture by the wearing of a head covering. Therefore a woman in the Corinthian church could only pray or prophesy if she demonstrated that she was under the leadership of the church, and she demonstrated this by wearing a head covering and by acting consistently with that principle.

d) **I do not permit**: The strength of Paul's wording here makes it challenging to obey this command in today's society. Since the 1970's, our culture has rejected the idea that there may be different roles for men and women in the home, in the professional world, or in the church. In this text (among others), the Holy Spirit clearly says there *is* a difference in roles.

   i. But the cultural challenge must be seen in its true context – not just a struggle between men and women, but as a struggle with the issue of authority in general. Since the 1960's, there has been a massive change in the way we see and accept authority. https://enduringword.com/bible-commentary/1-timothy-2/

Our culture has developed to the point where many of the above restrictions do not apply. However we can certainly agree that anyone who ministers must do so under the administration of their pastor, being decent and in order, following the precepts established by the gospel of our Lord and Savior Jesus Christ. The culture of the day in which Paul and Timothy ministered was engulfed with pagan cults and other forms of idolatrous worship. Some cults were female cults, where women lead and taught those specific beliefs; these were powerful cults with which many of those women would have been familiar and possibly even taken part. We are well aware of the struggles that the Gentile churches were enduring with the task of keeping the gospel pure. That was likely the impetus for such stern teachings in regards to the women at Ephesus. It should also be noted that women played significant roles in other pagan churches where they were under the administration of established leaders and had demonstrated fidelity to the gospel and their lives spoke to their integrity and charity.

Just what, then, did it take to be a leader in these Gentile churches? What qualified one for service? These qualifications are those which still serve as the framework for qualifications for church leadership in many congregations and this is due to the soundness of them. These qualifications are delineated for bishops, demons, and deacons' wives, the key leadership roles in congregations.

I Timothy 3:1 This is a true saying, If man desire the office of a bishop, he desireth a good work.

I Timothy 3:2 A bishop then must be blameless, the husband of one wife, vigilant, sober, of good behaviour, given to hospitality, apt to teach;

I Timothy 3:3 Not given to wine, no striker, not greedy of filthy lucre; but patient, not a brawler, not covetous;

I Timothy 3:4 One that ruleth well his own house, having his children in subjection with gravity;

I Timothy 3:5 (For if a man know not how to rule his own house, how shall he take care of the church of God?)

I Timothy 3:6 Not a novice, lest being lifted up with pride he fall into condemnation of the devil.

I Timothy 3:7 Moreover he must have a good report of them which are without; lest he fall into the reproach and the snare of the devil.

The responsibility of leading God's people is a life calling. What I mean by that is that every aspect of your life matters as the people of God are watching. Nothing can cause them to stumble - no indiscretion, so faux pas, no past slip ups, nothing. We all have a past and things happened. Honesty is the only policy when speaking about your past.

Your life while leading must bring honor to God and not shame.

I Timothy 3:16 And without controversy great is the mystery of godliness: God was manifest in the flesh, justified in the Spirit, seen of angels, preached unto the Gentiles, believed on in the world, received up into glory.

Godliness is what we strive to exemplify here on earth before God and men. Lord that we walk worthy of you.

<u>Reflection</u>

How does this nurturing tone of Paul's letter to Timothy impact your reading of it? Do you feel the same nurture for you and the ministry God has called you to ?

_____

_____

_____

_____

_____

_____

_____

_____

_____

_____

_____

_____

All Scripture

II Timothy 3:16

II Timothy 3:16 All scripture is given by inspiration of God, and is profitable for doctrine, for reproof, for correction, for instruction in righteousness:

True Edification for the Journey

The second epistle of Paul to Timothy is a bit more personal as it appears

Timothy needed to be reminded of who he was. Paul began by reminding

Timothy of his lineage of faith through his grandmother Lois and his mother Eunice. Sometimes we just have to be reminded of what exactly is in us. For Timothy, there was a wealth of faith on the inside, not to mention the gifts which he received when Paul laid hands on him. Oh, but there are real challenges that Timothy still has to face as he leads that church at Ephesus. How does Paul reassure the young man?

II Timothy 1:6 Wherefore I put thee in remembrance that thou stir up the gift of God, which is in thee by the putting on of my hands,

II Timothy 1:7 For God hath not given us the spirit of fear; but of power, and of love, and of a sound mind.

II Timothy 1:8 Be not thou therefore ashamed of the testimony of our Lord, nor of me his prisoner: but be thou partaker of the afflictions of the gospel according to the power of God;

II Timothy 1:14 That good thing which was committed unto thee keep by the Holy Ghost which dwelleth in us.

There were gifts on the inside of Timothy, that word of God and the ability to preach and teach with persuasion unto men. The testimony of Jesus Christ, that in him rests salvation and redemption, he had to share that testimony with boldness. Boldness even though there was the reality of imprisonment and the threat of all forms of persecution, even death. But

God had committed his gospel in his heart and in his mouth - the Holy
Ghost would continue to edify, lead, guide, direct, and speak peace to him.

Now, along with his own calling and gifting, he had to find others to preach and teach the gospel. The hardest realization was that persecution would come. Paul did not shield him from that very real possibility rather he put it before him and gave him hope. Keeping the purpose ever before him - it's for the eternal good of God's people. Ministers endure much for the sake of the people but we too have hope in our endurance.

II Timothy 2:10 Therefore I endure all things for the elect's sakes, that they may also obtain the salvation which is in Christ Jesus with eternal glory. II Timothy 2:11 It is a faithful saying: For if we be dead with him, we shall also live with him:
II Timothy 2:12 If we suffer, we shall also reign with him: if we deny him, he also will deny us:

For millions of people, believers in diverse places in this world today, the threat of death for naming the name Jesus Christ is still real. They need these same words of courage, strength, and edification. My God that they be strengthened in this very moment to endure what they must endure to your glory. That they claim you, own you, confess you regardless of what befalls them. My God, by your Holy Spirit, speak peace to endure and overcome in Jesus' precious name, Amen.

We must recognize how important study was and is to the body of Christ. If we do not equip ourselves with knowledge, knowing that eternity rests with what we say to men, we could cause many to miss glory. Lord keep me in your word, teach me, illuminate your word, that someone will hear and receive from your servant. Amen

II Timothy 2:15 Study to shew thyself approved unto God, a workman that needeth not to be ashamed, rightly dividing the word of truth.

II Timothy 2:16 But shun profane and vain babblings: for they will increase unto more ungodliness.

I need to be honest right here - there is nothing I detest more in ministry than an unprepared, unstudied, lazy preacher. They are an insult to our Lord. They stand and deliver nothing to people who are dying - disgraceful.

We can not afford to stand before the people of God, shucking and jiving, Sunday after Sunday. Eternity is in the balance and their blood is on their hands. God, awaken a sincere, insatiable hunger for your word in your people. Let them cry out for your word and those whom you have called to preach and teach your gospel. Amen

For the day is coming and is at hand when people will reject all that is godliness. They are in need now just as they were in Timothy's day. The world is so ugly, openly hateful, those who love genuinely are rare.

II Timothy 3:2 For men shall be lovers of their own selves, covetous, boasters, proud, blasphemers, disobedient to parents, unthankful, unholy, II Timothy 3:3 Without natural affection, trucebreakers, false accusers, incontinent, fierce, despisers of those that are good,

II Timothy 3:4 Traitors, heady, highminded, lovers of pleasures more than lovers of God;

II Timothy 3:5 Having a form of godliness, but denying the power thereof: form such turn away.

We have not changed very much over the centuries have we? These same things are still in the world. What a shame! And it would seem that they have gotten worse and worse but God is still God. The more we pour into our children the more they will be able to stand among their peers and be bold for Christ. They need to know. They cannot afford to sit in worship and bible study playing games and watching videos on their phones. They need to look up and live. Just as Lois and Eunice poured into Timothy, we are called to do the same in our families, communities, and congregations. We must be well equipped to teach and preach this word. Not some of the word, all of it.

II Timothy 3:16 All scripture is given by inspiration of God, and is profitable for doctrine, for reproof, for correction, for instruction in righteousness.

We present this gospel to the world just as Paul admonished Timothy. Stir up the gift which is on the inside of you. Go win someone to Christ!

Reflection

Have you considered how important having sound teaching and preaching are? Is one sufficient without the other? Explain.

_____

_____

_____

_____

_____

_____

_____

_____

_____

_____

_____

_____

The Provocation
Hebrews 3:16

Hebrews 3:16 For some, when they had heard, did provoke: howbeit not all that came out of Egypt by Moses.

The Heir of All Things

Hebrews is one of the most interesting books in the New Testament. The author is unnamed and the message is staggering as it seeks to bring Jewish converts back to their new found religion. It begins by making the connection between the prophets to whom the Jews would have been extremely familiar. He then goes on to point out that just as the prophets spoke to their ancestors the new testament was the incarnate word, Jesus Christ. It presents Christ as the savior who sits at the right hand of the Father and who is superior to the angels.

Hebrews 1:4 Being made so much better than the angels, as he hath by inheritance obtained a more excellent name than they.

Hebrews 1:5 For unto which of the angels said he at any time, THOU ART MY SON, THIS DAY HAVE I BEGOTTEN THEE? And again, I WILL BE TO HIM A FATHER, AND HE SHALL BE TO ME A SON?

In establishing the deity of Christ the author has shown a better path to righteousness by faith in Jesus Christ. There is a clear difference between the angels and Christ. Each has ministered to God's people but salvation comes only by Jesus Christ.

Hebrews 1:13 But to which of the angels said he at any time, SIT ON MY RIGHT HAND, UNTIL I MAKE THINE ENEMIES THY FOOTSTOOL?

Hebrews 1:14 Are they not all ministering spirits, sent forth to minister for them who shall be heirs of salvation?

The role of the angels in the lives of believers is critical - they minister to the saints as they are given charge to do so. And even though that is the case angels are not to be worshiped.

Jesus did that which none but he was able to do. He came from glory, through the lineage of men, took on our sins, died, rose, ascended, and now intercedes for us at the right hand of his Father. No angel was able to do that. Yes, he took on humanity, lowering himself, for the good of all mankind.

Hebrews 2:9 But we see Jesus who was made a little lower than the angels for the suffering of death, crowned with glory and honour; that he by the grace of God should taste death for every man.

Hebrews 2:17 Wherefore in all things it behoved him to be made like unto his brethren, that he might be a merciful and faithful high priest in things pertaining to God, to make reconciliation for the sins of the people. Hebrews 2:18 For in that he himself hath suffered being tempted, he is able to succour them that are tempted.

My Lord, the humility of Christ! To understand the magnitude of what he did for us - it takes your breath away. How he endured life as a man, to save us from our sin, and even now is still interceding for us because he understands. I mean really, he gets it. The temptations, the frustrations, the joys, the anguish, he truly gets us because he was like us with the exception of remaining sinless. Who better to stand between God and us pleading our case, asking mercy on our behalf. Lord, I thank you.

Gratitude should be the disposition of every believer. Christ has redeemed us from our sin and justified us by his blood. What more would need to be done for unbelievers to believe? That is the next question that this author addresses and he elicits the help of Moses and those who came out of Egypt to illustrate this point.

Hebrews 3:3 For this man was counted worthy of more glory than Moses, inasmuch as he who hath builded the house hath more honour than the house.

Hebrews 3:4 For every house is builded by some man; but he that built all things is God.

Hebrews 3:5 And Moses verily was faithful in all his house, as a servant, for a testimony of those things which were to be spoken after;

Hebrews 3:6 But Christ as a son over his own house; whose house are we, if we hold fast the confidence and the rejoicing of the hope firm unto the end.

Faith was being built in the Jews and they were falling away. This letter is a reminder of those things which they have already experienced as a people. They have experienced, again and again, the penalty of sin and faithlessness. Would they dare suffer these things again? The author reminds them of the Provocation, how when Moses ascended Mt. Sinai for them to the presence of God that they turned away from the God who had delivered them. Surely they could not within them the capacity to repeat an error of this magnitude? Yes, they did. With an opportunity like that which Christ had presented them the author hoped to persuade them by the example of the deaths of their ancestors because of the Provocation.

Hebrews 3:14 For we are made partakers of Christ, if we hold the beginning of our confidence stedfast unto the end;

Hebrews 3:15 While it is said, TO DAY IF YE HEAR MY VOICE , HARDEN NOT YOUR HEARTS, AS IN THE PROVOCATION.

Hebrews 3:16 For some, when they had heard, did provoke: howbeit not all that came out of Egypt by Moses.

Hebrews 3:17 But with whom was he grieved forty years? [was it] not with them that had sinned, whose carcases fell in the wilderness?

Hebrews 3:18 And to whom sware he that they should not enter into his rest, but to them that believed not?

Hebrews 3:19 So we see that they could not enter in because of unbelief.

As in the time of Moses there will be a faithful few who will remain faithful until the end. Salvation is available to all. Lord that all would receive this gift that came at so great a cost!

Reflection

Why do you believe so many do not receive this great gift of salvation? What more can be done to persuade them?

_____

_____

_____

_____

_____

_____

_____

_____

_____

_____

_____

_____

_____

Envying and Strife

James 3:16

James 3:16 For where envying and strife is, there is confusion and every evil work.

<u>Words of Edification</u>

Though there is some uncertainty as to the author of this letter it is primarily believed to have been written by James, the half brother of Jesus. The audience is the twelve tribes who are scattered abroad thereby making this a Jewish audience. And this letter, as are they all, is rich with spiritual wisdom that would lead to discernment. He truly seeks to edify those who are of the faith.

James 1:4 But patience have her perfect work, that ye may me perfect and entire, wanting nothing.

James 1:5 If any of you lack wisdom, let him ask of God, that giveth to all men liberally, and upbraideth not; and it shall be given him.

Two hard things right at the beginning, patience and wisdom. They are each sorely needed and required for this Christian journey, by my goodness, what it takes to gain them. And he goes even deeper by taking believers to the realm of temptation.

James 1:12 Blessed is the man that endureth temptation: for when he is tried, he shall receive the crown of life, which the Lord hath promised to them that love him.

James 1:13 Let no man say when he is tempted, I am tempted of God: for God cannot be tempted with evil, neither tempteth he any man:

James 1:14 But every man is tempted when he is drawn away of his own lust, and enticed,

James is calling believers to accountability for themselves and their sin. It was no doubt easy to shift blame then as it is now. Yet the truth of this word remains as well - You cannot be tempted unless that lust was already there. There are some things that could be presented to me and I would be like "Ok...and" but there are some others for which I would have to fight with myself. I know that so I avoid those things. I'm stronger than I was but I'm still a work in progress. If you're honest with yourself, and that is the key with this issue of temptation, you still have some growth points too.

What are believers called to confront next with this mirror James is holding up to their faces? Another hard issue - treatment of others. He puts forth an analogy of how a wealthy man would be treated in the assembly and how a poor man would be treated - clearly there are some stark differences. The one is esteemed and the other is despised. That is still prevalent today. I am reminded now of the story of a homeless man who often walked the streets of New Orleans, Magazine Street in particular near Austerlitz Street.

Everyone knew him and many folk often talked to him. I saw folks bring him food after church if he was around but it struck me that no one ever invited him into the church itself. Now there were no less than five churches in the vicinity and I assumed someone was inviting him in. Well, there was one weekend that was particularly cold for New Orleans, below freezing in fact with a little precipitation so that made that night seem even colder. I thought about the homeless that night but I had seen so many go into a nearby shelter so I assumed, as kids do, that everyone was safe and warm.

Wrong.

That following Sunday morning we were horrified to learn that Petey, that was his name, and his dog that he named after himself, Petey Jr., had both died of hypothermia during the night. He had not had anywhere to go that would allow Petey Jr. to stay with him so the two of them slept outside, in the freezing rain and sleet, and died. I felt sick and there are tears in my eyes over thirty years later as I recall that story. Where was the compassion of the church? Why did someone help? Sure he was dirty, probably intoxicated, the dog was dirty too but didn't they deserve compassion?

James 2:13 For he shall have judgment without mercy, that hath shewed no mercy; and mercy rejoiceth against judgment.

James 2:14 What doth it profit, my brethren, though a man say he hath faith, and have not works? Can faith save him?

James 2:15 If a brother or sister be naked, and destitute of daily food, James 2:16 And one of you say unto them, Depart in peace, be ye warmed and filled; notwithstanding ye give them not those things which are needful to the body; what doth it profit?

James 2:17 Even so faith, if it hath not works, is dead, being alone. James 2:21 Was not Abraham our father justified by works, when he had offered Isaac his son upon the altar?

James 2:22 Seest thou how faith wrought with his works, and by works was faith made perfect?

James 2:23 And the scripture was fulfilled which saith, Abraham believed God, and it was imputed unto him for righteousness: and he was called the Friend of God.

So, to be clear, the author is not suggesting here that the works alone earned Abraham the title of righteous. It was the fact that he was faithful - being willing to sacrifice Isaac - and put in the work to fulfill the sacrifice that proved just how much Abraham believed and trusted God. That was the work - going to that mountain, building that altar, talking Isaac up there, putting him on that altar, raising that knife to plunge it into his son's chest - that was the work. He trusted God explicitly - that was righteous.

Oh boy this next bit of instruction may be the hardest bit yet. What are we to do with the tongue? It is a wild, monstrous, fiery beast and sometimes I don't like mine at all. Sometimes I don't even know who it belongs to, just crass. But seriously, if we cannot control that little thing it will wreck a house, break people's spirits, decimate hopes, and shatter dreams. Now it can also speak life, kindle hope, spark joy, and flow with edification if you can control it.

James 3:5 Even so the tongue is a little member, and so boasteth great things. Behold, how great a matter a little fire kindleth!

James 3:6 And the tongue is a fire, a world of iniquity: so is the tongue among our members, that it defileth the whole body, and setteh on fire the course of nature; and it is on fire of hell.

James 3:10 Out of the same mouth proceedeth blessing and cursing. My brethren, these things ought not so to be.

It can bring about so much chaos to be so little. Truly we ought to mind our tongues far better than we do. And we should be careful to teach that spiritual principle to our children. Some of the most venomous tongues are forked and in the mouths of serpents - they're quite small and in the mouths of our children. They have sharp tongues and jealous hearts - some of those lessons were learned watching interactions within our churches.

James 3:14 But if ye have bitter envying and strife in your hearts, glory not, and lie not against the truth.

James 3:15 This wisdom descendeth not from above, but is earthly, sensual, devilish.

James 3:16 For where envying and strife is, there is confusion and every evil work.

James has taken the time to speak to the heart of believers. These teachings are the things that can tear down or build up a body of believers because the church is relational. If we cannot treat each other in love here on earth there should be no expectation of fellowship in glory.

Reflection

After reading these first three chapters, which of the instructions that James offered do you consider the truest challenge for you personally?

_____

_____

_____

_____

_____

_____

_____

_____

_____

_____

_____

_____

_____

A Good Conscience

I Peter 3:16

I Peter 3:16 Having a good conscience; that, whereas they speak evil of you, as of evildoers, they may be ashamed that falsely accuse your good conversation in Christ.

A New Heir to a Living Hope

The authorship of the letters attributed to Peter is in question for a couple of obvious reasons: this letter is addressed to Gentile churches and the apostle Peter is known to have been an apostle to Jewish converts; this congregation should have been written to by Paul or some of those who were under his leadership; and finally the difficulty of dating it seems to place it, because of the historical references in it, to after the death of Peter. Regardless of these difficulties the letter edifies the Gentile churches of Asia Minor who were clearly being subjected to persecution.

I Peter 1:3 Blessed be the God and Father of our Lord Jesus Christ, which acceding to his abundant mercy hath begotten us again unto a lively hope by the resurrection of Jesus Christ from the dead,

I Peter 1:4 To an inheritance incorruptible, and undefiled, and that fadeth not away, reserved in heaven for you,

I Peter 1:5 Who are kept by the power of God through faith unto salvation ready to be revealed in the last time.

The believers are reminded of the blessings that they will obtain because of their faith. It is their hope in an age of persecution. They are reminded that this gift of salvation is one which even the angels admire and are looking on. The necessity of their obedience is likewise pressed into their spiritual awareness. They have obtained a very precious gift through Jesus Christ, whom they have been preached, and they should walk worthy in those gifts.

I Peter 1:13 Wherefore gird up the loins of your mind, be sober, and hope to the end for the grace that is to be brought unto you at the revelation of
Jesus Christ;
I Peter 1:14 As obedient children, not fashioning yourselves according to the former lusts in your ignorance:

Everyone can acknowledge a time in their lives when they had no true knowledge of Jesus Christ. Life at that point in our existence was different because of our ignorance to the fact that there was so much more. We, like this congregation, had no true standard by which to live. But when Jesus became a part of our lives and we were indwelt by the Holy Spirit, change had to and did come.

I Peter 1:15 But as he which hath called you is holy, so be ye holy in all manner of conversation;
I Peter 1:16 Because it is written, BE YE HOLY; FOR I AM HOLY.

There is a great expectancy for the lives of the saints. That expectancy, to live holy because Jesus is holy, that will not change. How is this life of holiness possible? It is only possible by believers consciously making changes to how we live and by studying the word of God fervently.

I Peter 2:1 Wherefore laying aside all malice, and all guile, and hypocrisies, and envies, and all evil speakings,
I Peter 2:2 As newborn babes, desire the sincere milk of the word, that ye may grow thereby:
I Peter 2:3 If so be ye have tasted that the Lord is gracious.

One of my dear friends who is resting with the Lord, Rev. Dr. Robert Earl Houston, was known to say "The Lord is kind," and truly he is. He nourishes our spirit man with his word and when we are young in the faith, immature spiritually, he gives us "spiritual" milk. But as we mature we receive strong sustenance from the word; those lessons that ensure we are nurtured are provided to us by God's holy word. This is because all of us, from the inception of this Christian reality into the world, up to this generation, we are all precious in God's sight.

I Peter 2:9 But ye are a chosen generation, royal priesthood, an holy nation, a peculiar [**1519** *eis* (a preposition) – properly, *into* (*unto*) – literally, "*motion into which*" implying *penetration* ("unto," "union") to a particular *purpose* or *result*.] people; that ye should shew forth the praises of him who hath called you out of darkness into his marvelous light:
I Peter 2:10 Which in time past were not a people, but are now the people of God: which had not obtained mercy but have now obtained mercy.

God did a great work in the Gentiles, unifying them and us unto himself. Calling them and us all out of the darkness which was at one time all that we knew. We are truly peculiar, coming forth in these times, brought together by faith in one man and his once for all perfect sacrifice. Our very lives are made possible by this supreme act of obedience and love made incarnate, the word in the flesh, Jesus Christ.

And these peculiar people are given instructions, practical instructions, for living in a world from which they are very different. These instructions for wives and husbands are ageless. But how we are to be ready with a defense of our faith couldn't be more appropriate than it is right now.

I Peter 3:**1** Likewise, ye wives, [be] in subjection to your own husbands; that, if any obey not the word, they also may without the word be won by the conversation of the wives;
I Peter 3:**2** While they behold your chaste conversation [coupled] with fear.
I Peter 3:**3** Whose adorning let it not be that outward [adorning] of plaiting the hair, and of wearing of gold, or of putting on of apparel;

I Peter 3:**4** But [let it be] the hidden man of the heart, in that which is not corruptible, [even the ornament] of a meek and quiet spirit, which is in the sight of God of great price.

I Peter 3:**5** For after this manner in the old time the holy women also, who trusted in God, adorned themselves, being in subjection unto their own husbands:

I Peter 3:**6** Even as Sara obeyed Abraham, calling him lord: whose daughters ye are, as long as ye do well, and are not afraid with any amazement.

I Peter 3:**7** Likewise, ye husbands, dwell with [them] according to knowledge, giving honour unto the wife, as unto the weaker vessel, and as being heirs together of the grace of life; that your prayers be not hindered.

I Peter 3:**8** Finally, [be ye] all of one mind, having compassion one of another, love as brethren, [be] pitiful, [be] courteous:

I Peter 3:**9** Not rendering evil for evil, or railing for railing: but contrariwise blessing; knowing that ye are thereunto called, that ye should inherit a blessing.

I Peter 3:**10** For he that will love life, and see good days, let him refrain his tongue from evil, and his lips that they speak no guile:

I Peter 3:**11** Let him eschew evil, and do good; let him seek peace, and ensue it.

I Peter 3:**12** For the eyes of the Lord [are] over the righteous, and his ears [are open] unto their prayers: but the face of the Lord [is] against them that do evil.

I Peter 3:**13** And who [is] he that will harm you, if ye be followers of that which is good?

I Peter 3:**14** But and if ye suffer for righteousness' sake, happy [are ye]: and be not afraid of their terror, neither be troubled;

I Peter 3:**15** But sanctify the Lord God in your hearts: and be ready always to give an answer to every man that asketh you a reason of the hope that is in you with meekness and fear:

I Peter 3:16 Having a good conscience; that, whereas they speak evil of you, as of evildoers, they may be ashamed that falsely accuse your good conversation in Christ.

You just have to be sure that you have an answer because someone will be curious one day. Someone will ask you about your beliefs. Someone will be curious about your walk in life. They will want to know why you live how you live. There will be questions, some well-intentioned and some malicious, about this God we serve. Your answer should be as well known to you as your name is. That will not be the moment to struggle and come up with something that sounds good. Your answer must be honest and from your heart - Thy word, God, have we hid in our hearts that we might not sin against you or bring you shame...

<u>Reflection</u>

So what is your answer to why do you serve Jesus Christ?

_____

_____

_____

_____

_____

_____

What does he mean to you?

_____

_____

_____

_____

_____

_____

Know What You Know

II Peter 3:16

II Peter 3:16 also in his epistles, speaking in them of these things; in which are some things hard to be understood, which they that are unlearned and unstable wrest, as they do also the other scriptures, unto their own destruction.

Stir Up the Saints

Simon Peter take s this letter as an opportunity to stir up believers in their holy faith. We all need this from time to time as life can get us down. He reminds them that they have escaped the lusts of life and runs down a litany of qualities which they have also obtained by their faith.

II Peter 1:4 Whereby are given unto us exceeding great and precious promises: that by these ye might be partakers of the divine nature, having escaped the corruption that is in the world through lust.

II Peter 1:5 And besides this giving all diligence, add to your faith virtue; and to virtue knowledge;

II Peter 1:6 And to knowledge temperance; and to temperance patience; and to patience godliness;

II Peter 1:7 And to godliness brotherly kindness; and to brotherly kindness charity.

II Peter 1:8 For if these things be in you, and abound, they will make you that ye shall neither be barren nor unfruitful in the knowledge of our Lord Jesus Christ.

These characteristics mirror the heart and mind of Christ. These characteristics are to be exemplified in the body of Christ. However there are clearly examples of behaviors which should not be, and God's wrath will not be withheld from the unrighteous. We have become familiar with the idea of entanglements and how detrimental those can be. We would do well to remember that once we are freed from sinful entanglements we do not have to find ourselves entangled again.

II Peter 2:20 For if after they have escaped the pollutants of the worlds through the knowledge of the Lord and Savior Jesus Christ, they are again entangled therein, and overcome, the latter end is worse with them than the beginning.

II Peter 2:21 For it had been better for them not to have known the way of righteousness, than, after they have known it, to turn from the holy commandment delivered unto them.

IIn Peter 2:22 Bit it is happened unto them according to the true proverb, The dog is turned to his own vomit again; and the sow that was washed to her wallowing in the mire.

Not getting caught up in the way one used to live is so hard for many people. We're comfortable there, we know that kind of life. But it is always hard because it is uncertain. Even a new faith walk is very disconcerting because it is unknown. What do we do? We go back to what we know, no matter how dysfunctional it may have been. For with the promise of salvation came the promise of newness. Regardless of how long it may take, newness will come.

II Peter 3:9 The Lord is not slack concerning his promise, as some men count slackness; but is longsuffering to us-ward, not willing that any should perish, but that all should come to repentance.

God is yet calling for repentance, that turning away from our sin once we see it as God sees it. The concept is quite misunderstood, being thought of as an apology. That's not at all what it is. It's seeing sin as God sees it, hating it, and turning from it. He is waiting for us to repentant and come back to him. Repentance leads us to righteousness.

II Peter 3:14 Wherefore, beloved, seeing that ye look for such things, be diligent that ye may be found of him in peace, without spot, and blameless.

II Peter 3:15 And account that the longsuffering of the Lord is salvation; even as our beloved brother Paul also according to the wisdom given unto him hath written unto you;

II Peter 3:16 As also in all his epistles, speaking in them of these things in which are some things hard to be understood, which they that are unlearned and unstable wrest, as they do also the other scriptures, unto their own destruction.

The scriptures are not for casual reading. As you delve into them you should be intent on doing a study of them if it is your intention to understand. You've got to be willing to put in the work in order to see how to apply it to your life and receive the blessings.

Reflection

What has been most illuminating for you from II Peter? How can you apply that to your daily walk with Christ?

_____

_____

_____

_____

_____

_____

_____

_____

_____

_____

_____

_____

Perceive We the Love of God

I John 3:16

I John 3:16 Hereby perceive we the love of God, because he laid down his life for us: and we ought to lay down our lives for the brethren.

Fellowship with Him

John opens with the declaration of a profound truth - he is in fellowship with the Father and with Jesus Christ. The great news, this is not an exclusive fellowship as it is open to all who would receive it.

I John 1:6 If we say that we have fellowship with him, and walk in darkness, we lie, and do not the truth:

I John 1:7 But if we walk in the light, as he is in the light, we have fellowship one with another, and the blood of Jesus Christ his son cleanseth us from all sin.

Jesus is the light of the world and that light is within us. Evidence of that light is how we live our lives as if others don't see it - something is wrong with our walk. Now this light shouldn't only shine on Sunday, if it shines it shines always. The more mature you are in your faith the brighter your light should be.   Little light, little power. Bright light, much power. Sin deems that light if not snuffs it out completely.

I John 2:15 Love not the world, neither the things that are in the world. If any man love the world, the love of the Father is not in him;

I John 2:16 For all that is in the world, the lust of the flesh, and the lust of the eyes, and the pride of life, is not of the Father, but is of the world. I John 2:17 And the world passeth away, and the lust thereof: but he that doeth the will of God abideth forever.

We can be so attached to those things that we know, the worldly things. We deliver a love for those things and forget that they do not last forever. The tethers to this world are so strong but we must be willing to let go and cleave unto the things of God. God's promises are eternal. There isn't a single thing here on this earth that I esteem so highly that I would lose eternity in the presence of God for it. I say that without fear of contradiction. I have the hope of what is to come and it is this same hope that John longs to instill in the church.

The world can be so enticing but we are not loved by the world - they do not understand us.

I John 3:1 Behold, what manner of love the Father hath bestowed upon us, that we should be called the sons of God: therefore the world knoweth us not, because it knew him not.

I John 3:2 Beloved, now are we the sons of God, and it doth not yet appear what we shall be: but we know that, when he shall appear, we shall be like him; for we shall see him as he is.

On that day, the day of his return, we shall have the inheritance of the promise. All the challenges of our journey, and the journeys of all those who came before us will be worth it on that day when we shall see him and be like him. His love for us will be on full display for every eye to see.

I John 3:16 Hereby perceive we the love of God, because he laid down his life for us: and we ought to lay down our lives for the brethren.

Jesus being our perfect example laid down his life for us. We are admonished to have the mind of Christ, even to the point of death. Someone has been asked to do that today, as you are reading these pages. What if it was you? Would you give your life for another?

Reflection

Have you truly considered the depths of God's love for us? Take some quiet time today and just ponder that love.

_____

_____

_____

_____

_____

_____

_____

_____

_____

_____

_____

_____

Lukewarm

Revelation 3:16

Revelation 3:16 So then because thou art lukewarm, and neither cold nor hot, I will spue thee out of my mouth.

<u>Prophetic Words to the Churches of Asia Minor</u>

Each chapter in the book of Revelation is filled with a specific word of prophecy to each of the churches in Asia Minor. They are told of their good and their bad - this lets us know that churches are under the watchful eye of our Savior. Since our Lord is changeless, we must assume that we too are under his watchful eye. This book of prophecy must be the most feared and misunderstood book in all of sacred scripture. Is that because we assume that it is an enigma? Do we honestly believe that there is anything in God's word that he will not open to us if we ask? Some do sincerely believe that this book of Revelation is out of our depth. I say no. The word teaches us that if we lack wisdom we can ask of God and he will give it to us liberally. I asked and God poured in to me for this entire book that you hold in your hands. This is no different.

The Revelation is from Jesus Christ himself as he gave it to John. The Revelation was not for everyone but rather was intended for his servants and those who hear it. The Revelation is specifically addressed to the Seven Churches of Asia Minor - these are Gentile Churches.

Revelation 1:1 The Revelation of Jesus Christ, which God gave unto him, to shew unto his servants things which must shortly come to pass; and he sent and signified it by his angel unto his servant John:

Revelation 1:2 Who bare record of the word of God, and of the testimony of Jesus Christ, and of all things that he saw.

John is clarifying his position and purpose in Christ and for the Revelation which he is writing. John is the servant [1401] [doulos] - slave, bond servant in verse 2 who bears record [3140] [martureo] - to be a witness; give evidence of the word of God, the testimony [3141] [marturia] - evidence given of Jesus Christ, and those things which he saw [1492][eido] - to know; be aware; behold. John was an apostle who walked with Christ and was a part of his earthly ministry. He is uniquely qualified to be the vessel through which the Revelation pours forth into the world.

Revelation 1:3 Blessed is he that readeth, and that hear the words of this prophecy, and keep those things which are written there in.

Revelation 1:4 John to the seven churches which are in Asia: Grace be unto you, and peace, from him which is, and which was, and which is to come; and from the seven Spirits which are before his throne;

The reference in verse 4 is undoubtedly God almighty due to the allusion to his preeminence and eminence in the continuity of time. The seven Spirits [4151] [pneuma] - angels; like a current of air, Holy Spirit are before his throne.

Revelation 1:5 And from Jesus Christ, who is the faithful witness, and the first begotten of the dead, and the prince of the kings of the earth. Unto him that loved us, and washed us from our sins in his own blood,

Jesus is referred to as the first begotten of the dead [3498] [nekus] dead. I take this to mean that Jesus was the first divine immortal being who took on the form of mortal men and dwelt among us as a human being. He took on mortality to redeem us from our sins.

Revelation 1:6 And hath made us kings and priests unto God and His Father; to him be glory and dominion for ever and ever. Amen.

Then, in verse 8, Christ speaks.

Revelation 1:8 I am Alpha and Omega, the beginning and the ending, saith the Lord, which is, and which was, and which is to come, the Almighty.

As the second person of the Trinity, Christ is just as God is, existing within the continuity and fluidity of time. John tells his readers that he was on the isle of Patmos and in the Spirit on the Lord's day when he received the Revelation for the churches. From behind him he hears a voice that reminds him of the loudness of a trumpet.

Revelation 1:11 Saying, I am Alpha and Omega, the first and the last: and What thou seest, write in a book, and send it to the seven churches which are in Asia; unto Ephesus, and unto Smyrna, and unto Pergamos, and unto Thyatira, and unto Sardis, and unto Philadelphia, and unto Laodicea.

After receiving the command from Christ, John turns to look to see who is speaking to him. It is interesting that he does not recognize him as the same Jesus who walked the earth with him because he is in a divine form with hair described as white like wool, fiery eyes, feet that looked like fired brass, and a voice that sounded like running waters. More remarkable than all that is the things which were with him: seven stars in his right hand and a sharp two edged sword in his mouth. When John saw him, he passed out. I would have too. But he identified himself again in verse 17 saying, Fear not; I am the first and the last: No one else has ever relinquished their divinity and immortality as Christ did - He was the first and the last. Jesus begins to unfold the mystery as this chapter comes to a close.

Revelation 1:20 The mystery of the seven stars which thou sawest in my right hand, and the seven golden candlesticks. The seven stars are the angels of the seven churches: and the seven candlesticks which thou sawest are the seven churches.

Here's a quick word study for the sake of clarification:

Seven [2033] [hepta] seven
Stars [792] [aster] as strown over the sky; literally a star
Angels [32][aggelos]- a messenger, a pastor
Churches [1577][ekklesia] members on earth or saints in heaven or both
Candlestick [3087] [luchnia] a lampstand

As we have read the Pauline epistles and the letters of Peter, James, etc. it is abundantly clear that the churches of Asia had significant issues to overcome. There had been false prophets, lying teachers, the influences of paganism, and a falling away of the faithful as many feared for their lives due to persecution. Significant challenges to say the least.

Each church has a message just for them. Christ has seen them.

Ephesus had struggle with those who claimed to be apostles but were liars: Revelation 2:2 I know thy works, and thy labour, and thy patience, and how thou canst not bear them which are evil: and thou hast tried them which say they are apostles, and are not, and hast found them liars:

Revelation 2:3 And hast borne, and hast patience, and for my name's sake hast laboured, and hast not fainted.

The Ephesian church had endured so much and it was exhausting no doubt. When you try to trust people to be who they claim and they just aren't, that can cause you to lose faith in what they say they represent.

That is a probable cause for what Jesus says next.

Revelation 2:4 Nevertheless I have somewhat against thee, because thou hast left thy first love
Revelation 2:5 Remember therefore from whence thou art fallen, and repent, and do the first works; or else I will come unto thee quickly, and will remove thy candlestick out of his place, except thou repent.

I am reminded that Paul admonished the pastor of the Ephesian church Timothy, as he struggled to minister to the congregation. They were being torn apart by those who sought to build themselves and destroy the church. They had left their first love - the gospel. They were beginning to mix the gospel of Jesus Christ with other gospels. As Timothy sought help, he prayed for them, and preached, and taught and yet they were at this point. Jesus said that he himself would take the candlestick. A candlestick holds up the lit candles. The candlestick causes the light to be lifted up so that it can be seen. Without the light of theri first love, the gospel, truly they did not need to be lifting up and shining a false gospel into the world. He ends his message to them with a word of hope:

Revelation 2:7 He that hath an ear, let him hear what the Spirit saith unto the churches; To him that overcometh will I give to eat of the tree of life, which is in the midst of the paradise of God.

That is the blessing of eternal life to those who overcome. Amen.

The church at Smyrna had suffered similar challenges from those who claimed to be Jews but were of the synagogue of Satan. They too had tribulations, and poverty. He leaves them with this word of hope:

Revelation 2:11 He that hath an ear, let him hear what the Spirit saith unto the churches; He that over cometh shall not be hurt of the second death.
Another blessing of the inheritance of eternal life.

The church at Pergamos had not denied the faith in Christ even when martyrdom was near them, However they have allowed those in their midst who were of Balaam and who taught Balac, paganism,and the doctrine of the Ncolaitanes, which the Lord said he hates. They are told to repent of these sins to receive the promise:

Revelation 2:17 He that hath an ear, let him hear what the Spirit saith unto the churches; To him that overcometh will I give to eat of the hidden manna, and will give him a white stone, and in the stone a new name written, which no man knoweth saving he that receiveth it.

Manna was that food that sustained Israel during the Exodus. It was God given nourishment that required them to trust God daily to meet their needs. Likewise stones were often taken as memorials for the people to have tangible reminders of how God had kept them from hurt, harm, and danger.

The Thyatira church Jesus recognized for their works, patience, charity, service and faith. Regardless of all their good they had allowed in their midst a woman named Jezebel who called herself a prophetess and who had led many to sin. Jesus gave her an opportunity to repent and she did not and her punishment was allotted to her and her children. The promise for those overcomers was:

Revelation 2:26 And he that overcometh, and keepeth my works unto the end, to him will I give power over the nations:

To the church at Sardis he said that they had received the word, held fast to it, repented of their sin. They were told to be watchful and to strengthen those things which were dying. They are also told that some of them will walk with him in white because of their worthiness. Their blessing is:

Revelation 3:5 He that overcometh, the same shall be clothed in white raiment; and I will not blot out his name out of the book of life, but I will confess his name before my Father, and before his angels.

My Lord, what an awesome blessing - your name not only in the book of life but for Jesus himself to confess your name in the presence of God and angels!

To the church at Philadelphia he says he has set before them an open door - that door is salvation through him. It's open but they are weak, having only a little strength . He will cause unbelievers, even those of the synagogue of satan to worship at their feet. Their faithfulness will also keep them from temptation.

Revelation 3:12 Him that overcometh will I make a pillar in the temple of my God, and he shall go no more out: and I will write upon him the name of my God, and the name of the city of my God, which is new Jerusalem, which cometh down out of heaven from my God: and I will write upon him my new name.

Their promise is amazing as it extends to the world to come and their place and identity in it.

The Laodiceans have a dire message:
Revelation 3:15 I know thy works, that thou art neither cold nor hot: I would thou wert cold or hot.

Revelation 3:16 So then because thou art lukewarm, and neither cold nor hot, I will spue thee out of my mouth.

What an indictment from the Lord! To be spit out of his mouth because of mediocrity. My Lord that our worship would be true, our praise sincere, our study earnest, our preaching sound. Lord that we bring your name glory as we work charitably within the community. That we love each other with your love. Lord that you never speak this judgment against. This is the challenge. Churches are open everywhere and they "Do church as usual." They fail to realize that church is not something we do - the church is who we are.

Reflection

How has this portion of the book of the Revelation been opened in your understanding? What has it taught you about how important we are to Jesus?

_____

_____

_____

_____

_____

_____

_____

_____

_____

_____

_____

_____

_____

_____

Volume Two Reflection

What is the primary challenge in the New Testament?

_____

_____

_____

_____

_____

How does that challenge impact your Christian journey?

_____

_____

_____

_____

_____

_____

_____

WORKS CITED with Notes

Holy Bible. Authorized King James Version (1611)

Saint Joseph Edition of The New American Bible. New York: Catholic Book Publishing Company, 1970

Finley, Thomas J. "Zephaniah." The Apologetics Study Bible. Peabody, MA:Holman Bible Publishers, 2012 .

Strong, James LL.D. S.T.D. THE NEW STRONG'S EXHAUSTIVE CONCORDANCE OF THE BIBLE. Nashville, Tennessee: Thomas Nelson,Inc., 1990.

"Testimony, Tabernacle of." Bible Study Tools.com
https://www.biblestudytools.com/dictionary/testimony-tabernacle-of/
     Testimony, Tabernacle of the tabernacle, the great glory of which was that it contained "the testimony", i.e., the "two tables" (Exodus 38:21). The ark in which these tables were deposited was called the "ark of the testimony" (40:3), and also simply the "testimony" (27:21 ; 30:6).

"The Peace Offering." Ligonier Ministries.
https://www.ligonier.org/learn/devotionals/peace-offering/
     The peace offering was given under three circumstances — for thanksgiving, upon the payment of a vow, or as a free expression of the worshiper's goodwill (7:11–18). Freewill offerings were given in response to God's unexpected or unsought generosity. A vow offering was brought to celebrate an answer to prayer after a person vowed to praise the Lord if He answered the worshiper's prayer. The peace offering for thanksgiving is probably better translated as a "confession" or "praise" offering that was given when someone was in dire need of deliverance. All of these peace offerings are seen in Scripture. Hannah's lavish offering when she dedicated Samuel to the Lord is an example of a peace offering given to commemorate the payment of a vow (1 Sam. 1:21–28).

"The Regulative Principle." Ligonier Ministries.
https://www.ligonier.org/learn/devotionals/the-regulative-principle/

Many biblical texts clearly teach that our holy Creator takes His worship very seriously. In today's passage, for example, we read of the occasion on which God struck Nadab and Abihu dead for offering "strange fire" (Lev. 10:1–3). Commentators are not sure about the exact nature of their infraction, but they do agree that the seriousness of the offense is related to their worshipping God in a manner that He had not commanded. They sought to be innovators in worship, and they paid the price for it.

"Tribe of Benjamin: Characteristics, Symbol, & History." Study.com

https://study.com/academy/lesson/tribe-of-benjamin-characteristics-symbolhistory.html

It has long been said that those who live by the sword will die by the sword. Military victory and violence go hand-in-hand. Of the Twelve Tribes of Israel described in Judeo-Christian traditions, few may have understood this as well as the Tribe of Benjamin.In the scriptures, Jacob's twelve sons went on to found the Twelve Tribes of Israel and thus the first Israelite nation. Before he died, Jacob gave each son a prophetic blessing, describing them and the fate of their tribe. Of Benjamin, Jacob said: "Benjamin is a ravenous wolf, devouring the prey in the morning, and dividing the spoil at night."It's an interesting blessing; it indicates that Benjamin (and his people) would be fierce warriors. However, the prophecy also made clear that the tribe's existence would be one of perpetual violence, day and night.

"Jehoiakim." Jewish Virtual Library.

https://www.jewishvirtuallibrary.org/jehoiakim

JEHOIAKIM (Heb. יְהוֹיָקִים ,יְהֹיָקֵם; "YHWH raises up"), king of Judah (609–598 B.C.E.). Pharaoh Neco made Jehoiakim king of Judah after he captured *Jehoahaz, Jehoiakim's younger brother, who was the choice of the *am ha-areẓ and who reigned for only three months. Jehoiakim, who was 25 when he ascended the throne (according to I Chron. 3:15 he was the second son of Josiah), was most likely selected because of his known support of a pro-Egyptian policy. Jehoiakim's original name Eliakim was changed by the Pharaoh in order to indicate the Judahite king's subservience to Egypt (II Kings 23:34; II Chron. 36:4). Egypt also imposed a heavy tax on Judah – 100 talents of silver and a talent of gold – which Jehoiakim exacted by levying a tax upon all people of the land (II Kings 23:33, 35).

"Capital." Encyclopedia Britannica.

https://www.britannica.com/technology/capital-architecture

Capital, in architecture, crowning member of a column, pier, anta, pilaster, or other columnar form, providing a structural support for the horizontal member (entablature) or arch above. In the Classical styles, the capital is the architectural member that most readily distinguishes the order.

"Jachin and Boaz." Jewish Virtual Library.
https://www.jewishvirtuallibrary.org/jachin-and-boaz

JACHIN AND BOAZ (Heb. יָכִין בֹּעַז), two pillars which were set up in front of the Sanctuary in Solomon's Temple in Jerusalem (I Kings 7:15–22, 41–42; II Kings 25:13, 17; Jer. 52:17, 20ff.; II Chron. 3:15–17; 4:12–13). The form and nature of these pillars are uncertain, and many proposals have been advanced by scholars. There is a detailed description of the pillars in II Kings 7:15–22, 41–42 and II Chronicles 3:15–17; 4:12–13. The pillars were composed of two major parts: the stem, 18 cubits (c. 30 ft.) in height, five cubits (c. 8 ft.) in circumference, and one cubit in diameter; and the capital of the pillar, five cubits in height. The size of the capital was apparently altered in one of the renovations of the Temple, undertaken after the time of Solomon. Thus, in II Kings 25 the height is given as only three cubits. During the renovation all the pillars were apparently recast, which probably explains the contradiction between the description of the construction of the pillars in Kings and that in Jeremiah. According to the former, the pillars and their capitals were cast from solid copper (I Kings 7:16, 46), while according to the latter, they were hollow (Jer. 52:21)... The Septuagint in one passage (I Kings 7:21 [7]) reads the Masoretic Boaz as Baaz (also Boas), and in another (II Chron. 3:17), as an adverbial phrase, Ισχύς (be-oz, "with strength").

"Pomegranate: The Biblical Fruit of Knowledge." http://friendfiji.com/wp-content/uploads/2016/05/POMEGRANATE-The-bibli cal-fruit-of-knowledge-Fiji-Times-Online.pdf

Jewish tradition teaches that the pomegranate is a symbol for righteousness, because it is said to have 613 seeds that corresponds with the 613 mitzvot or commandments of the Torah. In some artistic depictions, the pomegranate is found in the hand of Mary, mother of Jesus.

Ecclesiastes 3:11

He hath made every [thing] beautiful in his time
https://www.biblestudytools.com/commentaries/gills-exposition-of-the-bible/ecclesiastes-3-11.html

Isaiah 1:8 Explication http://lavistachurchofchrist.org/LVanswers/2009/07-14c.html "Ezekiel's four Living Creatures." Lipnick, Jonathan. Israel Institute of Biblical Studies: July 25,2018.

https://blog.israelbiblicalstudies.com/holy-land-studies/ezekiels-four-living-creatures/ Ezekiel's Four Living Creatures By Jonathan LipnickJuly 25, 2018*5 comments*

The Book of Ezekiel is the third of the major prophetic books of the Hebrew Bible, following the books of Isaiah and Jeremiah. Ezekiel is a unique figure unlike most of the prophets, in that he delivered all his oracles outside the Land of Israel. He was active for roughly 25 years (593-571 BCE) as part of the community of exiled Judahites in Babylonia. Although he was not a firsthand witness,

Ezekiel lived through to the greatest disaster of Israelite history until that time: the total destruction of the city of Jerusalem in 586 BCE. We do not know anything about his life prior to the age of 30 when he received his first vision by the River Chebar in the Babylonian exile. In the year 593 BCE, he received his first vision: the Vision of the Chariot, also called the Vision of the Divine Throne...Note that Ezekiel is careful not to label these sacred figures as actual animals, only semblances of animals. He uses the term "something like" or in the Hebrew *demut* which means a "likeness" or "appearance." This word is used ten times in this vision. In Hebrew the "four living creatures" are *arba chayot*. The word *chaya* comes from the root חיה "to live" which is also the source of the Hebrew name חוה *Chavah* = Eve (Gen. 3:20). These are partly human, partly animal, bearing much in common with both the *seraphim* (Isa. 6:2) and the *cherubim* (1 Kgs. 6:23-28) charged with guarding the Holy of Holies within the Temple...

https://www.bible-studys.org/Bible%20Books/Joel/Joel%20Chapter%201.html

The book of Joel is penned by the prophet Joel. He was a prophet in Judah. The name "Joel" means Jehovah is God. Joel was trying to call the people to repent of their sins, and be brought back into good standing with God. The one message that really stands out in the book of Joel is "the Day of the Lord". Joel is unique in the fact of the promise of the outpouring of the Holy Spirit on all flesh.

Joel 1:1 "The word of the LORD that came to Joel the son of Pethuel."

"The word of the LORD": This introductory phrase is commonly employed by the prophets to indicate that the message was divinely commissioned (Hos. 1:1; Mic. 1:1; Zeph. 1:1). Slightly varied forms are found (in 1 Sam. 15:10; 2 Sam. 24:11; Jer. 1:2; Ezek. 1:3; Jon. 1:1; Zech. 1:1; Mal. 1:1).

"LORD": A distinctively Israelitish designation for God; the name speaks of intimacy and a relationship bonded metaphorically through the covenant likened to marriage and thus carries special significance to Israel (Exodus 3:14).

"Joel": His name means "the Lord is God."

"Pethuel": His name means "open heartedness of/toward God" and is the only occurrence of this name in the Bible.

There is very little known of Joel, the person. He was believed by many to be one of the earliest prophets in Judah. Notice again, this is the LORD's Word in the pen of Joel. There is nothing more known of Pethuel, than the fact that he is the father of Joel.

https://www.biblestudys.org/Bible%20Books/Nahum/Book%20of%20Nahum.html

Title: The book's title is taken from the prophet-of-God's oracle against Nineveh, the capital of Assyria. Nahum means "comfort" or "consolation" and is a short form of Nehemiah ("comfort of Yahweh"). Nahum is not quoted in the New Testament, although there may be an allusion to (Nahum 1:15 in Romans 10:15; Isaiah 52:7).

Author – Date: The author of the prophecy is named simply "Nahum the Elkoshite" (1:1), and all that is known of the prophet is gleaned from this prophecy. Probably the identity of the prophet is obscured so his message can be prominent. Nahum's mission was to comfort the kingdom of Judah, following the destruction of Israel by Assyria, by announcing God's coming judgment on Nineveh, the capital of Assyria. The purpose of Nahum's prophecy is twofold:

i   To deliver a message of judgment and destruction against Nineveh; and

ii   To give comfort to Judah, so recently ravaged by Assyria Since Assyria is doomed, it will constitute a threat no longer.

The prophecy of Nahum is dominated by a single idea, the doom of Nineveh. In describing this doom, Nahum writes lyric poetry of the highest quality. It has been called the most poetical of all the prophetic writings, and certainly is the most severe in tone of any of the Minor Prophets.

Historical – Theological Themes: Nahum forms a sequel to the book of Jonah, who prophesied over a century earlier. Jonah recounts the remission of God's promised judgment toward Nineveh, while Nahum depicts the later execution of God's judgment. Nineveh was proud of her invulnerable city, with her walls reaching 100 feet high and with a moat 150 feet wide and 60 feet deep; but Nahum established the fact that the sovereign God (1:2-5), would bring vengeance upon those who violated His law (1:8, 14; 3:5-7). The same God had a retributive judgment against evil which is also redemptive, bestowing His loving kindnesses upon the faithful (1:7, 12-13, 15; 2:2). The prophecy brought comfort to Judah and all who feared the cruel Assyrians. Nahum said Nineveh would end "with an overflowing flood" (1:8); and it happened when the Tigris River overflowed to destroy enough of the walls to let the Babylonians through. Nahum also predicted that the city would be hidden (3:11). After its destruction (in 612 B.C.), the site was not rediscovered (until 1842 A.D.).

Nahum, who penned this book, was a relative unknown. He was from Elkosh in Judah. The name "Nahum" means full of comfort. Nahum prophesied about the time of Jeremiah. Most scholars believe Nahum's prophecy began about 620 B.C. His message is that Nineveh will fall.

Soon after Nineveh repented at the preaching of Jonah, they fell back into their old sinful ways.

Nahum 1:1 "The burden of Nineveh. The book of the vision of Nahum the Elkoshite."

The prophecy is a message of doom. Nahum was only the messenger of this divine oracle of judgment on Nineveh. "Nineveh" was the Assyrian capital situated on the Tigris River. It fell to Babylon (in 612 B.C.; see note on Jonah 1:1-3). We immediately see that this message for Nineveh came to Nahum by a vision from God.

https://www.biblestudys.org/Bible%20Books/Habakkuk/Book%20of%20Habakkuk.html

Title: This prophetic book takes its name from its author and possibly means "one who embraces" (1:1; 3:1). By the end of the prophecy, this name becomes appropriate as the prophet clings to God regardless of his confusion about God's plans for His people.

Author – Date: As with many of the Minor Prophets, nothing is known about the prophet except that which can be inferred from the book. In the case of Habakkuk, internal information is virtually nonexistent, making conclusions about his identity and life conjectural. His simple introduction as "Habakkuk the prophet", may imply that he needed no introduction since he was a well known prophet of his day. It is certain that he was a contemporary of Jeremiah, Ezekiel, Daniel, and Zephaniah.

Because the prophet is known to us only by name once again indicates the relative unimportance of the prophet, the major importance of the prophecy, and, more importantly, the God who sends the prophecy. The prophet's name means "Embracer" or "A Wrestler," and this provides the key to the prophecy. The prophecy is a record of the prophet's wrestling with God in behalf of his people. Further, he embraced God by faith (chapter 3), and embraces his people giving them the message that after the judgment to come, Chaldea (Babylonia), will itself be judged. Because of the description (in 3:1; and the inscription in 3:19), some have inferred that Habakkuk was a Levite who assisted in the music of the temple.

The purpose of Habakkuk's prophecy is twofold:

 i To warn Judah of its coming judgment at the hands of Chaldea, and
 ii To comfort Judah concerning Chaldea's ultimate destruction.

The theme of the prophecy is judgment on Judah and Chaldea (Babylon).

The mention of the Chaldeans (1:6), suggests a late seventh century B.C. date, shortly before Nebuchadnezzar commenced his military march through Nineveh (612 B.C.), Haran (609 B.C.), and Carchemish (605 B.C.), on his way to Jerusalem (605 B.C.). Habakkuk's bitter lament (1:2-4), may reflect a time period shortly after the death of Josiah (609 B.C.), days in which the godly king's reforms (2 Kings Chapter 23), were quickly overturned by his successor, Jehoiakim (Jer. 22:13-19).

Historical Setting: Most commentators however, date Habakkuk's prophecy during the reign of King Jehoiakim. The fall of Nineveh occurred about (612 B.C.), in fulfillment of Nahum's prophecy. It may have been after this fulfillment that Habakkuk received his vision setting forth the overthrow of the Babylonian kingdom. If so, when Habakkuk prophesied, the southern kingdom was wallowing in its sin and tottering politically in view of the impending threat from Babylon, the current world power. Nebuchadnezzar may have already carried Daniel and many of

Jerusalem's nobles into captivity (in 605 B.C.), with the second deportation to soon follow (597 B.C.). The final destruction of the city was yet to occur (in 586 B.C.). Habakkuk's description of the Chaldeans and their feats many even allude to all three of these events. Putting the above considerations together, the date of Habakkuk's prophecy is somewhere between (655 B.C. and 598 B.C.). Advocates of the former view would select (655 B.C.), as the date of writing, which advocates of the latter view commonly select (606 B.C.).

The date of Habakkuk is difficult to ascertain, since he does not mention the king or kings during whose reigns he prophesied. The best key that Habakkuk offers for dating his prophecy is his description of the Chaldeans (in 1:5-11). Some commentators, noting that God says He is in the process of raising up the Chaldeans (1:6), would date the prophecy as early as the reign of Manasseh. Habakkuk's message therefore, would be that just as God raised up the Assyrians to judge Israel, so He is rising up the Chaldeans (Babylonians), to judge Judah. This interpretation would date the prophecy before the destruction of Nineveh, which resulted in the exaltation of the Chaldeans to world prominence.

Background – Setting: The prophecy of Habakkuk is unique among all prophetic literature. Overall, it contains a high caliber of Hebrew poetry. The first two chapters constitute a dialogue between the prophet and the Lord concerning the invasion of the Chaldeans (1:1-11), and their destruction (1:12 - 2:20). Chapter 3 is a psalm with instructions given to the musicians for its rendering (3:1, 19). In the first two chapters the prophet contends with the Lord and in the third chapter he submits to the Lord.

https://www.biblestudys.org/Bible%20Books/Zephaniah/Book%20of%20Zephaniah.html

      Title: As with each of the 12 Minor Prophets, the prophecy bears the name of its author, which is generally thought to mean "the Lord hides" (compare 2:3).

Author – Date: Three other Old Testament individuals share his name. He traces his genealogy back 4 generations to King Hezekiah (ca. 715 –

686 B.C.), standing alone among the prophets descended from royal blood (1:1). Royal genealogy would have given him the ear of Judah's king, Josiah, during whose reign he preached.

The prophet himself dates his message during the reign of Josiah (640 – 609 B.C.). The moral and spiritual conditions detailed in the book (compare 1:4-6; 3:1-7), seem to place the prophecy prior to Josiah's reforms, when Judah was still languishing in idolatry and wickedness. It was (in 628 B.C.), that Josiah tore down all the altars to Baal, burned the bones of false prophets, and broke the carved idols (2 Chron. 34:3-7).

While other prophets gave their pedigrees (Isa. 1:1; Jer. 1:1; Joel 1:1; Zech. 1:1), none goes into such great detail as Zephaniah, whose lineage shows that he was the great-great-grandson of good King Hezekiah. Zechariah traces his lineage back to his grandfather (Zech. 1:1). Thus the prophet is a descendant of the royal line, which makes his rebuke of princes and nobles all the more significant (1:8, 13, 18). By giving his lineage and citing King Josiah, during whose reign he ministered, Zephaniah linked himself with the godly kings and the godly remnant of Israel's history. Zephaniah ministered several decades after Nahum and was an early contemporary of Jeremiah. Zephaniah has been called "the orator" because of the oratorical style evident throughout the prophecy. Zephaniah has some literary affinities with Isaiah, but more with Jeremiah and Joel. Both he and Joel paint very dark pictures of the Day of the Lord, but in both books beautiful rays of light penetrate the darkness. Two recurring expressions are important:

i. "Remnant" (1:4; 2:7, 9; 3:13); and
ii. The "Day of the Lord" (1:7-10, 14-16, 18; 2:2-3; 3:8, 11, 16).

The purpose of Zephaniah's prophecy is to set forth what the Day of the Lord will mean to ungodly Judah, to the world powers (1:2 – 3:7), and to the godly remnant (3:8-20). His theme is the Day of the Lord, which destroys the false remnant of Baal (chapter 1), destroys the God-rejecting nations (Chapter 2), and purifies the true remnant (3:8-20).

https://www.biblestudys.org/Bible%20Books/Malachi/Book%20of%20Malachi.html

The Lord repeatedly referred to His covenant with Israel reminding them, for His opening words, of the unfaithfulness to His love/marriage relationship with them. God's love for His people pervades the book. Apparently the promises by the former prophets of the coming Messiah who would bring final deliverance and age-long blessings, and the encouragement from the recent promises of Haggai and Zechariah, had only made the people and their leaders more resolute in their complacency. They thought that this love relationship could be maintained by formal ritual alone, no matter how they lived. In a penetrating rebuke of both priests and people, the prophet reminds them that the Lord's coming, which they were seeking, would be in judgment to refine, purify and purge. The Lord not only wanted outward compliance with the law, but an inward acceptance as well. The prophet assaults the corruption, wickedness and false security by directing his judgments at their hypocrisy, infidelity, compromise, divorce, false worship and arrogance. Malachi set forth his prophecy in the form of a dispute, employing the question and answer method. The Lord's accusations against His people were frequently met by cynical questions from the people. At other times, the prophet presented himself as God's advocate in a lawsuit, posing rhetorical questions to the people based on their defiant criticisms.

Malachi indicted the false priests and the people on at least 6 counts of willful sin:

i   Repudiating God's love (1:2-5);
ii   Refusing God His due honor (1:6 - 2:9);
iii   Rejecting God's faithfulness (2:10 - 16);
iv   Redefining God's righteousness (2:17 - 3:6);
v   Robbing God's riches (3:7-12);
vi   Reviling God's grace (3:13-15).

There are three interludes in which Malachi rendered God's judgment:

i   To the priests, (2:1-9);
ii   To the nation (3:1-6);
iii   To the remnant (3:16 - 4:6).

Stewart, Don. Who Is the Angel of the Lord in the Old Testament?

https://www.blueletterbible.org/faq/don_stewart/don_stewart_26.cfm

Though all the good angels are angels of God, or angels of the Lord, there is one special angel who is distinct and unique from all the other angels, he is called the "angel of the LORD."

In Both Testaments
The Bible, in both testaments, speaks of this personage called the "angel of the LORD," the "angel of the Presence" or the "angel, or messenger, of the Covenant." He appears in many important contexts in Scripture. The manner in which he is described sets him apart from all the other angels.

Three Possibilities
Three major views have been put forth as to the exact identity of the angel of the LORD.

i   A mighty angel who acted as the special representative of the LORD.
ii   God the Father assuming a human body.
iii   God the Son, taking a body for a short period of time.

Each of these three views has its supporters. To determine which view best fits the evidence, we will consider some of the major appearances of the angel of the LORD and make some observations about those appearances

https://www.blueletterbible.org/faq/don_stewart/don_stewart_27.cfm

What does John 2:14 mean? https://www.bibleref.com/John/2/John-2-14.html

Sheep101.http://www.sheep101.info/sheepbible.html#:~:text=The%20prominence%20of%20sheep %20in,and%20Cain%20worked%20the%20soil.

GALATIANS 3 – THE CHRISTIAN, LAW, AND LIVING BY FAITH.

https://enduringword.com/bible-commentary/galatians-3/#top

https://www.blueletterbible.org/faq/don_ste wart/don_stewart_27.cfm